RAIL CENTRES:
OXFORD

RAIL CENTRES:
OXFORD

LAURENCE WATERS

IAN ALLAN LTD

LONDON

Sources and Acknowledgements

Information on much of the early history of the railway has been found in the following locations:

The Local History Library, Oxford
The Bodleian Library, Oxford
The Oxfordshire County Records Office
Public Records Office, Kew
BTHR Porchester Road, London
Great Western Society Museum, Didcot
The Oxford University Railway Society collection.

Other sources have been: *Trains Illustrated*, *Railway World*, Ian Allan Library, *Railway Magazine*, *Locomotive Review*, *County of Oxford* magazine, *Bradshaws Guides*, *The Oxford Mail and Times*, *Jacksons Oxford Journal*, *Journal of Transport History*, as well as many timetables and trade directories.

I would like to thank the following individuals who have contributed photographs and information on the local railway scene:

B. Matthews, A. Doyle, R. Simpson, P. Clark, D. Holmes, D. Shewry, M. Tasker, J. True, T. D. Stoyel, E. Mountford, J. B. Latham, R. Bowen, D. Tuck, G. Lockwood, D. Castle, W. Turner, B. Higgins, J. D. Edwards, R. Carpenter, J. Loader, E. Eggleton, D. Pye, G. Hine, F. Snow, S. Boorne, D. Kozlow, R. McAvoy, D. Parker, A. Simpkins, Dr G. Smith, J. Coiley, J. H. Bird, M. Mensing, Lens of Sutton and the Locomotive Club of Great Britain.

Special thanks are due to:

Colin Harris of the Bodleian Library, Oxford
Malcolm Graham and his staff at the Local History Library, Oxford
J. Wilber-Wright for his excellent diagrams
Linda Castell for deciphering my original writing and
Andria Fowler for producing the final copy
Andrew Fox of Ian Allan Ltd

And last but not least, the following current BR and ex-GWR employees who have supplied much information: P. Jones, J. Trethewey, S. Worsfold, J. Church, N. Butchers, L. Cross, T. Harris, C. Turner, J. Hubbard and to the present Area Manager, David Mather and his staff.

To Carol and Tim

Front Endpaper:
'Saint' class 4-6-0 No 2933 *Bibury Court* passes Kennington with the 12.10pm Paddington-Oxford semi-fast on 1 November 1951.
R. H. G. Simpson

Rear Endpaper:
Rebuilt 'West Country' Pacific No 34097 *Holsworthy* restarts the 12.15pm Washwood Heath-Eastleigh freight from the up loop north of Oxford station on 11 May 1963.
Gerald T. Robinson

First published 1986

ISBN 0 7110 1590 2

Published by Ian Allan Ltd, Shepperton, Surrey; and printed by Ian Allan Printing Ltd at their works at Coombelands in Runnymede, England

Photographs from the Locomotive & General Railway Photographs collection appear courtesy of David & Charles Ltd.

Right:
'Castle' class No 5071 *Spitfire* leaves Oxford with the up 'Cathedrals Express', passing a '2800' class 2-8-0 on a down freight in September 1959.
J. A. Coiley

Contents

Introduction

When you think of Oxford, what does the name conjure up? The University, founded in 1214 and renowned today as one of the greatest educational institutions in the world? The city itself, possibly one of the most beautiful in Western Europe? Or the industrial Oxford represented at Cowley, which for many years was the home of the Morris car, a name now swallowed up by the British Leyland giant? Possibly Oxford means one or all of these things to many people, but to many generations of older railway enthusiasts the mention of Oxford will conjure up visions of endless numbers of steam trains, queueing up to pass through this railway bottleneck, hauled by locomotives which represented all of the 'Big Four' railway companies, on a regular basis.

All of this came to an end when steam left the area during 1966, but today's enthusiast is still well catered for with the large variety of different locomotive types that can still be seen on a regular basis hauling the constant procession of freightliners, car, oil and coal trains which together with the cross country and InterCity passenger services still make Oxford a busy and interesting Rail Centre.

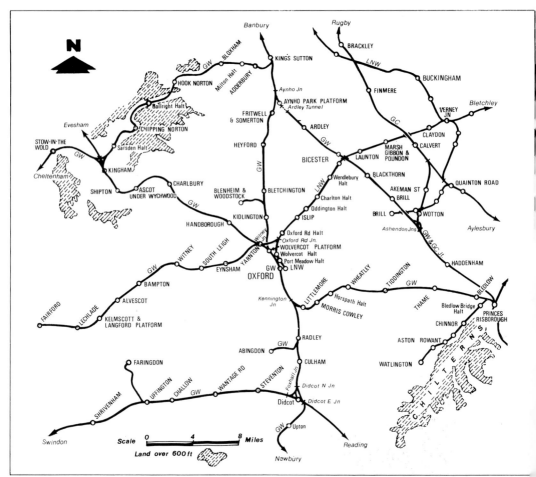

Early History

Much has been written regarding the formation of the Great Western Railway and its ambition to build a railway linking London and Bristol. This ambition was, of course, fulfilled by the opening of the line between these two points during 1841. It is interesting to note, however, that the company considered Oxford important enough as a potential railway centre to be included as a possible branch line in its original 1833 prospectus.

At this time Oxford had a municipal borough population of about 22,000, and the Great Western Railway obviously foresaw great potential in both freight and passenger traffic to and from this historic university city, but it was Brunel in particular, who probably viewed the line to Oxford as the first steps of a broad gauge gateway to the Midlands. However, when the building of the line from London to Bristol was started during 1836 it was to be without the Oxford branch, and it was another eight years before Oxford eventually got its railway.

The first really positive proposal for an Oxford branch had been included in the Great Western Railway directors' half-yearly report for 1836, which states: 'A Branch to Oxford and continuation of it to Worcester are promoted by the leading interests of those two cities, and the best exertions of the Company will be devoted in co-operation with them to accomplish those objects'. The Worcester portion was quietly dropped and in 1837 a bill for an Oxford Railway was promoted. The original draft proposal was for a line from a junction at Didcot northwards to Oxford crossing the River Thames twice and running into the city approximately parallel to the Cowley Road, terminating in a field adjacent to Magdalen Bridge. At this time (1837) the present Cowley Road was no more than a muddy lane flanked by open fields. Strong objections to this proposal were raised by the major landowners, Christ Church College, which forced Brunel to alter the route into the city. The new revised route envisaged the line entering the city to the east of the Abingdon Road and terminating on land near Folly Bridge. This time the University did not object,

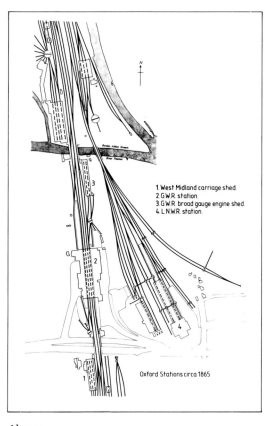

1. West Midland carriage shed.
2. G.W.R. station.
3. G.W.R. broad gauge engine shed.
4. L.N.W.R. station.

Oxford Stations circa 1865

Above:
The two stations at Oxford c1865.

but two of the principal landowners, who between them owned over half of the land required did, and once again the Oxford Railway was halted. Unperturbed, the Great Western Railway tried again in 1838 and again in 1840 to promote an Oxford branch but, as before, various objectors overruled their plans.

Up to this time people wishing to travel from Oxford were able to use the many stagecoach services. London was particularly well served with the top service being provided by the 'Rival Coach' which ran from the Angel Inn, High Street, to the Bell, Ludgate Hill at a fare of just 5s. By 1838 the GWR had extended its line as far as Steventon, and travellers from Oxford now only had to travel the 10 miles to the new railway, where they could then catch a train to London. Up to eight stagecoaches a day and a considerable amount of freight traffic made its way along the narrow road between Oxford city and Steventon station. The stagecoach journey, it is recorded, took 1½ hours and cost 3s. A census taken in 1842, showed some 77,567 passengers and 12,620 tons of freight were transported from Steventon station, a considerable amount of this traffic originating from the Oxford area. This importance was to be short lived, however, as in 1842 a new proposal for a railway to Oxford was made by the Oxford Railway Co with considerable support from the GWR. This time objections were few and the University was generally in favour of the line, but only after the railway had given assurances regarding the carriage of junior members. The University objected to any member below the status of MA travelling on the railway, and proctors were to be given free access to the stations to check on this. This curious state of affairs had arisen because of reports to the University authorities regarding the number of 'young gentlemen' using the nearby station at Steventon to travel to the races at Ascot.

One notable objector to the building of the line was the Warden of Wadham College, not, however, objecting on behalf of the college but as Chairman of the Oxford Canal Co. The Oxford Canal ran from Hawkesbury near Coventry to New Road Wharf, Oxford, a distance of 71 miles. Work started on its building in 1769 and finished on 1 January 1790. It connected with the Coventry and Ashby Canals, the Grand Junction and the Warwick & Napton, with a connection to the Thames at Oxford. From its opening the tonnage of goods carried together with the receipts had shown a continuous growth, so it was not unexpected that the Canal Co should complain about the possibility of railway competition.

For once all of these objections were overruled and after three previous abortive attempts, royal assent was obtained on 11 April 1843. This was for the building of a broad gauge line from a junction at Didcot, northwards for a distance of some 9 miles 57 chains to a field close by Folly Bridge in an area known as Grandpont.

On 31 August 1843 the Directors of the newly-formed Oxford Railway Co called an extraordinary general meeting of its share-holders at Paddington Station. At this meeting a Mr F. Barlow was elected Chairman of the

company and together with his fellow directors, Robert Gower, Thomas Guppy and Henry Simmonds, were able to report that all of the £120,000 share issue for the building of the railway had been taken up (much of this coming from the Great Western Railway, of course). Mr Thomas Osler was appointed company secretary at a salary of £200 per annum and after various resolutions were discussed and passed, the meeting was closed with a final resolution stating:

'That at the extraordinary and special general meeting of the company to be held this day it be recommended to make a sale of the Oxford Railway Company to the Great Western Railway upon their undertaking to defray all the expenses or charges incident thereto and being subject to the several agreements made by or on behalf of this Company.'

Below:
This map shows the 1844 Oxford Railway station at Grandpont. The small building to the bottom of the picture is actually the station; the larger is the goods shed. It is interesting to compare this plan with the Measham drawing of the station.
Courtesy Oxford County Libraries

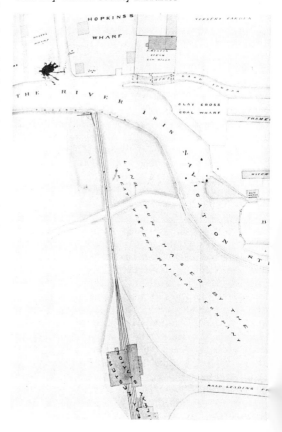

Work was begun on the line during October 1843, and with the help of a mild winter was completed by June 1844. After inspection by Brunel and the Government Inspector of Railways, the line was duly opened to traffic on Wednesday 12 June, 1844. A station was also opened at Didcot to serve the new branch.

The line itself ran northward from Didcot Junction, crossing the River Thames at Appleford and again at Nuneham, both of these crossings being by timber viaducts. Two intermediate stations were provided, one at Appleford Crossing (two miles north of Didcot) and the other at Abingdon Road (three miles north of Didcot). This latter station was renamed Culham in 1856 on the opening of the Abingdon Railway. On the outskirts of Oxford the line crossed the main Turnpike Road to Abingdon and then ran parallel to this road until reaching the terminus which was situated a short distance south of the Thames near Folly Bridge. Initially the line crossed the Abingdon Turnpike Road on the flat, but this crossing was soon replaced by a road bridge (known locally as the Redbridge). The delay over the building of this bridge was caused by a Mr Johne Towle, the occupier of the land, who, on hearing that a bridge was to be built on this plot, erected a temporary structure made from timber and brown paper which he purported to be a house in order to obtain extra compensation from the railway!

A few days prior to the public opening of the railway, a special train was formed to carry a party of about 50 notables, which included the Government Inspector of Railways, Maj-Gen Paisley, Charles Saunders, Secretary of the GWR and Brunel himself. It is reported that a satisfactory run was made, Didcot (53 miles from Paddington) being reached in 1hr 8min. The party arrived at Oxford around 2pm in good spirits and were taken by stagecoach to the Angel Inn, High Street, for a celebratory luncheon.

The opening of the line to the public on 14 June 1844 saw much rejoicing with great crowds gathering, especially in areas adjacent to the railway. In Hinksey field and South Hinksey a special gala day took place with marquees, tents and exhibitions set up for the opening; parties and celebrations, it is reported, went on late into the evening.

The first public timetable shows 10 trains a day in each direction, the first train leaving for London at 7.50am with the first arrival at Oxford from London being at 8.10am. It was to be quite a number of years before the railway gained prominence over the stagecoach service to London, as the early rail fares were certainly not cheap, at 15s, 10s and 6s respectively for each class to London. Local advertisements at this time proclaimed that it was possible to travel in style by 'Charles Holmes' and his splendid greys for only 5s. Eventually, however, the shorter journey times and greater comfort of the railway sounded the death knell of the horse-drawn coach on the London route.

The new terminus station provided at Oxford was a mainly wooden structure with an overall roof, containing two tracks, with small

Great Western Railway Time Table.

*Trains marked thus, * convey Third Class Passengers also.*

UP TRAINS.

Hrs. Mts.		Hrs. Mts.	
2 20 a. m.	Mail	2 45 p. m.	Express Train, calling only at Didcot.
7 50 a. m.		2 45 p. m.	
9 0 a. m.		4 0 p m.	
10 45 a. m.	Day Mail	*4 0 p. m.	
*10 45 a. m.		5 50 p. m.	
11 45 a. m. to meet Down Day Mail from Didcot.		8 0 p. m.	
12 55 p. m.			

DOWN TRAINS.

*9 0 a. m. to meet the	7 30 a. m. from London.				
11 45 a. m.	———	10 15 a. m.	———		
*12 55 p. m.	—— –	12 0 a. m.	———		
2 45 p. m.	———	2 0 p. m.	———		
5 50 p. m.	———	4 45 p. m.	———		

Passengers going by the 8 o'Clock Up Train from Oxford can avail themselves of the 8 55 p. m. from London—waiting at Didcot about two and a half hours.

ON SUNDAYS.

Up Trains—2 20 a. m. Mail ; 7 20 a. m.; 10 45 a. m. Day Mail ; *10 45 a. m. ; 5 50 p. m.

Down Trains—*7 20 a. m., meeting the 6 30 a. m. from London, and 10 45 a. m., meeting the Down Day Mail.

Coaches and Omnibuses.

Daily, from the Angel and Mitre Offices, High Street, and the Star Office, Cornmarket Street, unless otherwise expressed.

To London, *the Blenheim*, at half-past 10 a. m., through Wycombe, Uxbridge, &c., to the George and Blue Boar, Holborn, and Moore's, Green Man & Still, Oxford street.

London, *the Prince of Wales*, at half-past 10 a. m., from the Three Cups, Queen street, through Wycombe, Uxbridge, &c., to the King's Arms, Holborn hill.

London, *the Rival*, at 1 p. m., from the Vine, High street,

killed on the spot. It appears that these two men, with six others, were employed in hoisting with a crane two large trees, which were floating in the River Isis adjoining, and which were to be conveyed by rail. The men had succeeded in raising one tree and placing it in the truck, and were about raising the second, when, in spite of their combined efforts to swing it in the direction they required, it suddenly rebounded and striking with great force a portion of the crane, the shaft was driven out of its position, the supports gave way, and the whole fell in pieces. The porters hearing a crash endeavoured to get out of the way, and all succeeded in doing so, except Batts and Gardener, who were struck to the ground by one of the broken pieces supporting the crane. Batts was killed on the spot, his head being literally smashed; but Gardener, whose injuries were internal, survived a few minutes. Both bodies were conveyed to the Elephant and Castle, in St. Aldate's Street to await the coroner's inquest.'

In 1844 the Oxford & Rugby Railway Co had been formed to construct a line from Oxford via Fenny Compton to connect with the LNWR at Rugby. Royal assent was soon obtained and the work was started in 1846. Progress was slow, due to many financial problems, and by the time the line was completed to Banbury in 1850, control of the company had passed into the hands of the GWR.

The Birmingham & Oxford Junction Railway had also obtained an Act in 1846 to construct a line from Fenny Compton to Birmingham, a distance of 42¾ miles. This Act contained a clause that allowed the shareholders to lease their line to the GWR provided that four-fifths of them agreed. The LNWR acted quickly and in order to prevent the GWR obtaining control of the line and competing with their own Birmingham & London Railway, obtained many of the shares in an attempt, of course, to block this four-fifths agreement. A long drawn out battle resulted in an enquiry into the legality of this action, and eventually in 1848 the courts gave judgement in favour of the GWR. Almost immediately the Birmingham & Oxford Junction Co was taken over by GWR, and a decision was soon made not to build the last portion of the old Oxford & Rugby route

wagon turntables situated at the terminus ends; a further three tracks ran alongside this layout serving a large goods shed which was situated behind the terminus station. A single track continued for approximately 400yd to the river bank; here stood a small loading jetty together with a crane.

This station only remained open to the public for eight years and information regarding it is sparse, but an interesting mention is to be found in *Jacksons Oxford Journal* of 19 September 1846, from which this extract is taken:

'Fatal Accident at the Oxford Railway Station
Two Lives Lost

'On Saturday evening last, about seven o'clock, a dreadful accident occurred at the Oxford Station of the Great Western Railway, and we deeply regret to state that two of the porters employed by the Company, named Isaac Batts and Jas. Gardener, were

from Fenny Compton to Rugby, but instead to reach the Midlands using the later Birmingham & Oxford route via Fenny Compton and Leamington.

The new extension was initially built as a single track broad gauge line 24½ miles long to Banbury. Provision was made at the time for the eventual doubling of the track, and this gradually took place as the line was extended further northwards to Birmingham. As this second track was laid, mixed gauge was introduced throughout. At Oxford ballast for the new extension was obtained from nearby fields situated between the old terminus and the new line at Hinksey. This left a large area that soon filled with water, thereby forming Hinksey Lake. Many generations of fishermen have good reason to thank GWR for this action as it has become one of the best fishing spots in Oxford.

Initially trains travelling to and from the north from Oxford old station had to reverse at Millstream Junction to gain access to the new line, but this rather inconvenient manoeuvre ceased after 1 October 1852 when a new station at Oxford was opened approximately one mile northwards from Millstream Junction at the site which is still used today. The old terminus closed to passengers but continued to be used as a goods station until November 1872.

One interesting bonus which the new station gave to passengers was that they no longer had to cross a tollbridge to gain access to the station. At this time to cross Folly Bridge required payment of a toll, so passengers travelling from Oxford city had this extra charge to contend with. The new station was, however, positioned on the city side of the Osney tollbridge, thereby allowing free access to the site for city dwellers.

The opening of the new line to Birmingham on Friday 1 October 1852 meant that at last the Great Western Railway had gained a foothold in the Midlands. The line had a rather inauspicious start when on the day before the official opening a special directors' train hauled by the locomotive *Lord of the Isles* with Gooch himself on the footplate, collided with a goods train at Aynho. Luckily there were no serious injuries, and it is recorded that the passengers, greatly delayed, 'proceeded to the Royal Hotel Leamington where they took dinner'.

Trains over the new line were timed at 2¾hr for the 129 miles from Paddington to Birmingham Snow Hill, stopping only at Oxford and Leamington; unfortunately the autumn of 1852

Below:
Railways near Oxford, with railmotor halts, c1910.

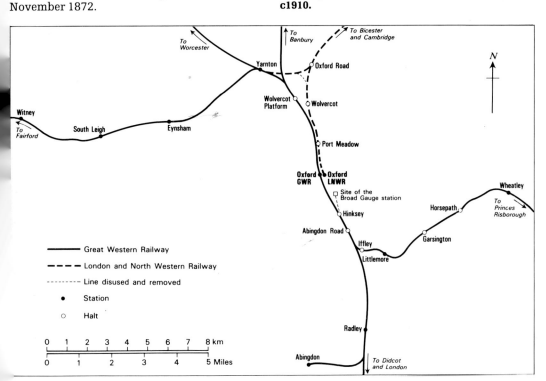

**This view illustrates the flooding at the station
area in 1875. The punt to the left was used to
ferry passengers to the GWR station, which at
this time was still provided with an overall roof.
This can be seen clearly in the right
background.** *Minn collection Bodleian Library*

was the wettest for some years, causing severe
flooding which was to play havoc with the
services. At Kennington, a very low lying area,
the line was flooded to such an extent that the
trains could not pass. A Board of Trade report
of 4 November 1852 describes just how the
railway operations were disrupted.

'On the evening in question the trains from
London were unusually late. The delay was
caused at Oxford in consequence of the floods
from the very great quantity of rain which had
fallen having rendered a portion of the line
impassable for engines, in consequence of
which it was necessary to draw the trains
through the water by means of horses. The
trains from London were stopped at Kennington Crossing between two and three miles
south of the Oxford station and about a
quarter of a mile south of the water. The
engine was here shifted to the rear of the
carriages, which it pushed to the water's edge;
horses were then harnessed to them, and the
carriages drawn by them through the water. At
the other side, the engine which was to take
the train on from Oxford was waiting; this
engine was accompanied by a pilotman, who
received his instructions from an Inspector of
Police, who was stationed on the south side of
the water. The actual time required to pass a
train through the water was about 12min.'

It was to be quite a few years before the
railway improved the drainage around the
line, as similar floods occurred in both 1875
and 1894. The 1875 flooding was so severe it
also affected the area at the station, as the
following report indicates.

'The heavy and continuous rain of last
Saturday (13 November 1875) had the effect of
causing a rapid rise in both the valleys of the
Thames and the Cherwell, and for miles the
country on Sunday morning was in some
places inundated to a much greater depth than
has been known almost within the memory of
man, and more than in the great flood of
1852 . . . St Thomas's, Osney, and all the
low-lying places were flooded to a considerable distance on each side between nine and
ten feet, thus rendering the road impassable.

'A punt was used at first for the conveyance
of passengers by train to the station, but on
Monday blocks of timber were laid down to
enable passengers to get to the up-platform.

'The traffic along the Botley Road had to go

Terrible Accident
ON THE
GT. WESTERN RAILWAY,
NEAR OXFORD,
On the 24th of December, where upwards of THIRTY PERSONS were KILL'D and more than Seventy Injured!

Above:
A newspaper report on the Shipton-on-Cherwell accident of 24 December 1874. *Author's collection*

Below:
The broad gauge locomotive *Snake* photographed at Oxford old station in 1865. Built by the Haigh Foundry in 1838 it was extensively altered by the GWR for working on the Oxford line, and was eventually withdrawn in 1869.
Minn collection Bodleian Library

over the Railway crossing, and the sight altogether was a very extraordinary one, hundreds of people being congregated on the spot looking at it. The water in the tunnel under the station was several feet in depth, and the wooden flooring was torn from its position and floating on top.'
(*Jacksons Oxford Journal*, 20 November 1875.)

During the 1880s the line was raised in the worst areas and with improved drainage of areas adjacent to the track, the flooding problem was solved.

In 1853 the Oxford, Worcester & Wolverhampton Railway was completed as a mixed gauge line, 89 miles long. It reached Oxford by way of a junction some three miles north of Oxford at Wolvercote. Permission had been given by the GWR for the OW&WR trains to traverse the GWR tracks for these three miles to reach Oxford station. The OW&WR Company had been promoted in 1843 to counteract the monopoly of the London & Birmingham Railway to the Midlands. This proposal had strong support from the GWR who actually provided six of the 16 directors initially appointed for the Company. Brunel himself was the engineer for this line and he obviously saw this proposal as a good chance to extend his broad gauge northwards from Oxford to

Above:

This picture shows Handborough station around the turn of the century; originally known as Handborough Junction when the OW&WR operated its service from Worcester to Euston in 1854. Here trains would connect to the GWR line via Wolvercot Junction and Oxford. A small refreshment room was built at this time to deal with the increased patronage.

L&GRP (6239)

Worcester and beyond, but various clauses were incorporated into the Act which provided for a mixed gauge to be built, thereby thwarting his dream. The broad gauge, although built in places, was never to be used.

The OW&WR was beset with problems from the start, the first of which was a wild underestimation as to the cost of the line by Brunel himself. His original estimate was £1½ million, but the true sum soon proved to be nearer £2½ million, and the first of many subsequent disagreements between the OW&WR and the GWR broke out. Money became short and the constant bickering and arguing between the two companies manifested itself in 1849 with a total deadlock, finances almost gone and not one mile of the 89 miles ready to open. After many court battles the situation was partly resolved and the OW&WR proceeded to try and complete the line. Extensive flooding during 1852 together with subsidence problems at Campden Tunnel

further delayed this, until at last the final section of the line was completed, and opened to the public on 4 June 1853 as a single mixed gauge line from Evesham to Wolvercot Junction. Gradually this last section of track was doubled until by 1858 the whole of the Southern section from Evesham to Wolvercot Junction was completed to mixed gauge. At this time there was no mixed gauge track south of Oxford, so the OW&WR, who did not operate broad gauge trains, were denied access to the south with their standard gauge services.

This situation partially resolved itself in 1854 when a standard gauge connection was completed between the OW&WR at Yarnton and the Buckinghamshire Railway at Oxford Road Junction. This 1½ mile connection was known as the 'Yarnton Loop' and gave direct standard gauge access to the LNWR line to Bletchley and southwards to Euston. This connection had been made possible by the building of a line by the LNWR under the guise of the Buckinghamshire Railway from Bletchley to Oxford in 1851. The OW&WR was quick to exploit the new connection and from 1 April 1854 a new through service from Worcester to Euston was inaugurated with up to four trains a day making the journey; the fastest time for the 129½ miles was around 4hr. This service completely avoided Oxford but a connecting train was provided at Handborough Junction, with a local service via Wolvercot Junction to

Oxford. For a few years a short connecting spur known as the 'South-West Junction' was provided between Yarnton and the LNWR line at Wolvercote to allow the OW&WR direct access to Oxford Rewley Road station, but this was little used and eventually taken out in 1863. With the opening of the Witney Railway in 1861 a new station was provided at Yarnton, and Handborough lost its junction status.

As already mentioned, the LNWR had gained access to Oxford in 1851 by way of the Buckinghamshire Railway Co Act of 1847. This provided for a line from Bletchley to a junction at Verney where one line ran northwards to Banbury and another southwards to Oxford. The Banbury section was the first to open on 1 May 1851, and subsequently the second part of the branch to Oxford was opened on 20 May 1851. This terminated on a site at Rewley Road, Oxford, where Rewley Abbey, a Cistercian monastery dating from 1287, once stood. Here a rather elegant terminus station was erected. An unusual aspect of the rail access to the site was the provision of a swing bridge to cross the Rewley Abbey stream known at this time as the Sheepwash Channel, which ran just north of the terminus.

In December 1856, mixed gauge lines were opened between Oxford southward to Reading West Junction and Basingstoke, thus allowing standard gauge trains to work 'through' from the north. By 1861 the main line pattern in Oxford was almost completed with the opening in October of that year of the mixed gauge extension from Reading to Paddington. This now gave the West Midland Railway, as the OW&WR had now become, standard gauge access to London via Oxford. Subsequently the longer service from Worcester to Euston via the Yarnton loop was discontinued in September 1861.

On 1 October 1861 a new standard gauge service was inaugurated between Paddington and Worcester via Oxford and the WMR, also to Wolverhampton and Birkenhead via Oxford, Banbury and Birmingham. The first standard gauge train from Paddington to Oxford, the 9.35 to Birkenhead was hauled by locomotive No 75, a 2-2-2 built by Beyer Peacock for the GWR in 1856. Arrival at Oxford was some 5min late; here the locomotive was changed to No 76 of the same class and, despite some fine running, the train's arrival at Birmingham was about 3min late. Hardly a good start to the standard gauge service!

Broad gauge trains continued to run northwards through Oxford but rarely further than Leamington, and by the mid-1860s most passenger trains were in the hands of standard

Below:
The OW&WR timetable of April 1854 shows just five trains per day in each direction with connections at Worcester for Wolverhampton. It would take a passenger on average four hours to complete the 91 miles from Oxford to Wolverhampton. The GWR route to Birmingham at this time took something under 2½ hours for the 66-mile journey. *Author's collection*

OXFORD, WORCESTER, & WOLVERHAMPTON.

FROM OXFORD. WEEK DAYS. SUN.

Dis Mls.	STATIONS.	1 2 & 3 Class	1 & 2nd Class.	1 & 2nd Class	1st & 2nd Class.	1st & 2nd Class	1st & 2nd Class.	1 2 & 3 Class
		A. M	A. M	P. M	P. M.	P. M	A. M	P. M
0	Oxford	8 25	11 10	1 20	4 20	6 55	7 30	6 5
7¾	Handborough	8 40	11 30	1 35	4 40	7 15	7 50	6 20
13¾	Charlbury	8 55	11 45	1 50	4 55	..	8 2	6 35
17½	Ascott	9 0	..	..	5 5	..	8 6	6 46
18½	Shipton	9 10	..	2 0	5 10	7 40	8 20	6 50
24½	Addlestrop	9 30	..	2 15	5 25	..	8 35	7 5
28¾	Moreton	9 40	12 10	2 25	5 35	7 55	8 47	7 17
32	Blockley	9 48	..	2 35	5 43	..	8 56	7 26
34	Campden	9 55	..	2 40	5 50	..	9 1	7 31
38¾	Honeybourne	10 5	..	..	6 0	..	9 14	7 44
43¾	Evesham	10 15	12 35	3 0	6 10	8 25	9 25	7 55
57¼	Worcester	11 0	1 5	3 40	7 0	8 50	10 0	8 30
80	Dudley	12 25	2 10	5 0	8 20	10 0	11 25	9 50
91	Wolverhampton	12 50	2 25	5 25	..	10 20	11 50	10 10

FROM WOLVERHAMPTON. WEEK DAYS. SUN.

Dis Mls.	STATIONS.	1 & 2nd Class	1 2 & 3 Class	1 & 2nd Class	1st & 2nd Class.	1st & 2nd Class.	1 2 & 3 Class.	1st & 2nd Class.
		A. M.	A. M.	A. M.	P. M	P. M.	A M.	P. M.
0	Wolverhampton	..	8 0	9 50	1 20	4 20	8 0	4 45
6	Dudley	6 30	8 30	10 25	2 0	4 40	8 30	5 15
33½	Worcester	7 30	9 55	12 0	3 10	5 40	9 55	6 40
17¼	Evesham	8 0	10 25	12 35	3 40	6 10	10 25	7 10
52½	Honeybourne	..	10 37	12 47	3 50	..	10 37	7 22
57	Campden	..	10 52	1 0	4 5	..	10 50	7 35
59	Blockley	..	10 58	1 5	4 10	..	10 55	7 40
62¼	Moreton	8 30	11 7	1 15	4 18	6 40	11 3	7 48
66½	Addlestrop	..	11 17	1 25	4 28	..	11 15	8 0
72¼	Shipton	8 45	11 32	1 35	4 40	6 57	11 30	8 15
73½	Ascott	..	11 37	..	4 45	..	11 35	8 20
77¼	Charlbury	8 55	11 45	1 50	4 55	..	11 45	8 30
83¼	Handborough	9 10	12 0	2 0	5 10	7 15	11 57	8 42
91	Oxford	9 35	12 20	2 20	5 3	7 25	12 15	9 0

ORDINARY FARES ON THE OXFORD, WORCESTER, AND WOLVERHAMPTON.

FARES FROM OXFORD TO

Station	Fares
Handborough	1s 9d 1s 2d 7½d
Charlbury	3s 2s 2d 1s 2d
Ascot	3s 10d 2s 8d 1s 5½d
Shipton	4s 2s 10d 1s 7d
Addlestrop	5s 3d 3s 8d 2s 0½d
Moreton	6s 2d 4s 4d 2s 5d
Blockley	6s 10d 4s 10d 2s 8d
Campden	7s 2d 5s 1d 2s 10d
Honeybourne	8s 3d 5s 9d 3s 3d
Evesham	9s 2d 6s 5d 3s 7½d
Worcester	12s 8s 6d 4s 9d
Dudley	14s 9s 9d 6s

Above:
When the Oxford Railway opened in 1844, two intermediate stations were provided: a small halt at Appleford Crossing and a much more substantial station called Abingdon Road, which was renamed Culham in 1856. Seen here in 1919, the Brunel-designed waiting room and booking office can be clearly seen on the up platform.
L&GRP (8431)

gauge locomotives. The end of the broad gauge north of Oxford came on 1 November 1868, when broad gauge working was removed from the timetable between Oxford and Birmingham; the track was removed the following year. The end was now in sight for the broad gauge in the Oxford area and on 25 November 1872 Oxford saw its last broad gauge train depart southwards, the track being removed by the end of the year. The old terminus at Grandpont used as a goods depot from 1852 had never been converted to mixed gauge and was therefore closed completely on 26 November 1872. The land not being required by the railway was sold for housing development and by 1880 all trace of the old station had disappeared.

In 1865 Oxford almost attained even greater importance as a railway centre with the proposal by the GWR to build a carriage works. In an arrangement with the local corporation the GWR had agreed to lease 22 acres of land at Cripley Meadow for the proposed carriage works site. The GWR favoured Oxford because of its central position and its mixed gauge track; the Council were interested because of the new jobs and prosperity that it would generate locally. Unfortunately the one body that did not want the works was the University, still a very powerful landowner at that time, and very soon a propaganda war was waged against the Council and the GWR with articles appearing in *The Times* and other national papers, with headlines such as 'The GWR Vandals and Oxford'. Many handouts stating the University's case against the works were also distributed to any parties interested in suppressing the works. Eventually the situation resolved itself in 1866 when Gooch, who had been elected Chairman of the GWR in March of that year, announced that the new works would be placed at Swindon.

Top right:
The broad gauge engine *Flirt* one of Gooch's 0-6-0 'Standard Goods' built at Swindon in May 1852. This particular engine, together with several others of the same type, was working from Oxford during 1862. *L&GRP (4756)*

Right:
Abingdon station in 1865 with the broad gauge still very much in evidence. The engine is one of the 'Leo' class of 0-6-0 saddle tanks built in 1842 to a Gooch design. *Courtesy Abingdon Museum*

Left:
'Queen' class 2-2-2 No 1128 *Duke of York* built in 1875, shown here as rebuilt in 1897. This particular locomotive was allocated to both Oxford and Fairford between 1904 until withdrawn in April 1914, being the last 'Queen' class locomotive to run. In 1906 it was fitted with ATC apparatus for working on the Fairford branch. *L&GRP (16060)*

Bottom left:
This photograph shows some of the Oxford GWR station staff during the early 1920s.
Courtesy D. Mather

Below:
A 'Queen' class 2-2-2 No 1132 *Prince of Wales* at the north end of the up platform at Oxford just after the turn of the century. *R. Carpenter*

This was a purely financial decision and was certainly not prompted by the University's objections. The land offered at Oxford was prone to considerable flooding in winter and it would have cost the GWR a considerable sum of money to alleviate the problem. The cost of building the works at Swindon was to be only half of that estimated for Oxford, so the situation was soon resolved and the academic tranquility of Oxford remained undisturbed.

The rail growth in the area was finally completed with the opening of two new lines which, although not close to Oxford, were to have a profound effect on the local railway scene. The first of these was the GW/GC connection from Culworth Junction on the Great Central Railway to Banbury Junction on the GWR which was opened for goods and passenger traffic in August 1900, thereby allowing through trains from the north-east and Yorkshire direct access to the south via Banbury and Oxford.

The growth of these services over the ensuing years saw Oxford become notorious as an operational bottleneck. This situation was slightly eased by the completion of the line from Ashendon Junction to Aynho. This was opened on 4 April 1910 and provided a much shorter direct route from Paddington to Birmingham, and as a result many of the Paddington-Birmingham trains were removed from the Oxford line.

The Great Western Branch Lines

The Abingdon Railway

The oldest local branch line was that of the Abingdon Railway Co.

The first positive steps to build a railway at Abingdon came with the 1837 proposal for the Oxford Railway which provided for a branch to Abingdon, but because of objections from the local MP, Mr Duffield, and some local councillors, the proposal was dropped and it was to be almost another 20 years before Abingdon became a railway town.

A second proposal in 1855 proved successful and a 1¾ mile single broad gauge line was duly constructed from a junction on the Oxford-Didcot line at Nuneham to a small terminus station at Abingdon: this was opened on 2 June 1856. The branch left the Oxford line just to the north of the river at Nuneham. A small wooden interchange station was provided at this point and was named Abingdon Junction: from here the line passed over flat country to terminate in Abingdon adjacent to Stert Street.

The station at Abingdon at this time consisted of a single platform with an overall roof and small wooden and brick booking office at the terminus end. A goods yard was provided, together with a stable for the delivery horses used by the railway. Provision was also made for the servicing of the branch engine with a small engine shed and watering facilities. This continued to be used until it was closed on 20 March 1953. The branch was then worked on the one engine in steam principle with servicing being undertaken at Oxford. A coal yard was soon established on the site which continued to be used until a few months before the line finally closed in 1984.

The early passenger service ran between the terminus and the interchange station, until the Didcot-Oxford line, together with the Abingdon branch, were converted from broad to standard gauge in November 1872. In 1873 the junction at Nuneham was taken out and the line extended northward for approximately ¾ mile alongside the main line to a newly constructed junction station at Radley. This station contained two main platforms with the Abingdon Bay situated on the down side, forming an island platform. A footbridge connected this to the up side, where the main station entrance and buildings stood. The small signalbox at Radley controlled the branch sidings and stood at the end of the up platform. The new service was inaugurated on 8 September 1873, with 10 trains a day each

Right:
This interesting picture shows the aftermath of the accident at Abingdon on 22 April 1908. The four-wheel coach has caused considerable damage to the station buildings, which resulted in their subsequent demolition and rebuilding.
Courtesy Abingdon Museum

Below:
Abingdon branch timetable for June 1876.
Author's collection

ABINGDON BRANCH—Worked by Train Staff.
Form of Staff and Ticket, SQUARE; Colour, VARNISHED OAK.

Distance	Single Line. STATIONS.	DOWN TRAINS.—WEEK DAYS.										NARROW GAUGE.						SUNDAYS.							
		1 Pass.	2 Pass. and Goods	3 Pass.	4 Pass. and Goods	5 Pass.	6 Pass.	7 Pass.	8 Pass.	9 Pass.	10 Pass.	11 Pass.	12 Pass.	13 Pass.	14 Pass. and Goods	15 Pass.	16	1 Pass.	2 Pass.	3 Pass.	4 Pass.	5 Pass.	6	7	8
		A.M.	A.M.	A.M.	A.M.	A.M.	A.M.	P.M.	P.M.	P.M.	P.M.	P.M.	P.M.	P.M.	P.M.	P.M.		A.M.	P.M.	P.M.	P.M.	P.M.			
	Radley	7 23	7 55	8 15	9 25	10 45	12 25	1 20	3 5	4 25	5 40	6 40	7 25	8 50	9 25	10 20	..	11 37	1 15	4 25	5 20	8 15	.	.	.
2¾	Abingdon	7 30	8 5	8 23	9 35	10 55	12 35	1 30	3 15	4 35	5 50	6 50	7 35	9 0	9 35	10 30	..	11 47	1 25	4 35	5 30	8 25	..	..	..

Distance	Single Line. STATIONS.	UP TRAINS.—WEEK DAYS.										NARROW GAUGE.						SUNDAYS.							
		1 Pass.	2 Pass.	3 Pass.	4 Pass.	5 Pass.	6 Pass.	7 Pass.	8 Pass. and Goods	9 Pass.	10 Pass.	11 Pass.	12 Pass. and Goods	13 Pass.	14 Pass. and Goods	15 Pass.	16	1 Pass.	2 Pass.	3 Pass.	4 Pass.	5 Pass.	6	7	8
		A.M.	A.M.	A.M.	A.M.	A.M.	A.M.	P.M.	P.M.	P.M.	P.M.	P.M.	P.M.	P.M.	P.M.	P.M.		A.M.	P.M.	P.M.	P.M.	P.M.			
	Abingdon	7 5	7 35	8 35	9 5	10 25	11 35	1 0	2 30	4 0	5 20	6 10	7 5	7 50	9 5	10 0	..	11 17	12 55	4 5	5 0	7 55	.	.	.
2¾	Radley	7 15	7 45	8 43	9 15	10 35	11 45	1 10	2 40	4 10	5 30	6 20	7 15	7 57	9 15	10 10	..	11 27	1 5	4 15	5 10	8 5	.	.	.

way, and with only slight variations to the timetable, continued to run until passenger services were withdrawn on 9 September 1963. The line continued to operate for freight only, but its future took a dip in 1980 when the nearby MG car plant closed (for many years MG cars had been shipped from Abingdon by rail). With the car traffic gone, the end finally came when Charrington's coal yard closed in June 1984. British Rail ran their customary last day special passenger train; a three-car DMU performed the final rites on 30 June 1984, and Abingdon lost its railway after 130 years of operation.

Throughout its existence the line has had a rather uneventful history but in 1865 the local council, who in 1837 had initially rejected the building of the railway, surprisingly offered some 20 acres of land adjacent to the line free of charge to the Great Western Railway in the hope that the company would place its proposed carriage works at Abingdon. Needless to say, the Great Western Railway declined the offer, probably as the land offered spent most of the winter severely flooded, to a

depth of 3ft in some parts.

In 1908 the terminus station at Abingdon was partially demolished; not by design, however, as a goods train being shunted in the yard unfortunately collided with some empty carriages standing in the station. It pushed these up into the terminus building, causing the roof partially to collapse. This building, already in a poor state of repair, was subsequently removed together with the overall platform roof, and was replaced with a new more substantial structure. This was built in English Bond brickwork with a slate roof and a rather splendid round pediment containing the station name. The new terminus building survived until well after passenger trains had ceased to run to Abingdon but was unfortunately removed by British Rail in the early 1970s.

Since its closure various schemes have been put forward to retain a rail link to Abingdon, including plans for a narrow gauge tourist line, but as the whole of the station area and yard is scheduled for redevelopment, this seems unlikely.

Motive Power

On the opening of the branch in June 1856 the Great Western Railway allocated the engine *Eagle* to work the first trains. This broad gauge 2-2-2 engine was built by Sharp Roberts in 1838. The Gooch registers indicate that it worked on the branch for about three years, being replaced in turn by engines *Venus* and *Atlas*; the latter engine being withdrawn in 1872 was probably the last broad gauge engine to work on the branch.

Standard gauge days saw a succession of small tank engines working the branch trains. '517' class 0-4-2T locomotives worked the service almost exclusively from 1872 to 1947: in fact, No 1159, a locomotive built in 1876,

Above:

This rare picture shows ex-Monmouthnshire Railway and Canal Co 4-4-0T No 1306 complete with the Abingdon branch set of four-wheel stock at Radley station. The locomotive was built as MR&CC No 15 in 1872 and was taken into GW stock on 1 June 1880, subsequently being rebuilt at Swindon in 1896. This locomotive was allocated to Oxford during 1901. *L&GRP (18221)*

Below:

The excellent station at Abingdon which was provided by the GWR in 1908 after the earlier structure was demolished. This photograph taken just after World War 1 shows the enamel advertising signs to good advantage.
Courtesy Abingdon Museum

Above:
Abingdon station yard on 28 July 1959, where 0-4-2T No 5818 shunts the local goods ready for its trip to Hinksey yard. *J. D. Edwards*

Below:
'Hall' No 4997 *Elton Hall* moves swiftly through Radley with an up freight on a bright February day in 1959. *J. D. Edwards*

Above:
Radley station looking south. 'Grange' class No 6851 *Hurst Grange* leaves for Oxford with a train of suburban stock. The Abingdon branch bay stands to the right of the picture. The date is 27 February 1959. *J. D. Edwards*

Right:
Timetable issued for the opening of the Witney Railway in November 1861. *Author's collection*

WITNEY RAILWAY.

ON AND AFTER THURSDAY, NOV. 14, 1861,
THE

WITNEY RAILWAY
WILL BE

OPENED
FOR PASSENGER TRAFFIC,

AND TRAINS WILL RUN AT THE FOLLOWING TIMES:

UP TRAINS.

Distance from Witney.	STATIONS.	1 & 2 Class. a.m.	1 & 3 Class. a.m.	1 & 2 Class. p.m.	1 & 3 Class. p.m.	FARES FROM WITNEY.		
Miles.						1st Class.	2nd Class.	3rd Class.
	WITNEY .	8 15	11 0	4 50	7 35	s. d.	s. d.	s. d.
2½	SOUTH LEIGH .	8 22	11 7	4 57	7 42	0 7	0 5	0 4
4½	EYNSHAM .	8 30	11 15	5 5	7 50	1 0	0 9	0 6
8½	YARNTON .	8 40	11 25	5 15	8 0	1 10	1 4	0 11
11½	OXFORD .	8 50	11 35	5 25	8 10	2 6	1 9	1 3

DOWN TRAINS.

Distance from Oxford.	STATIONS.	1 & 2 Class. a.m.	1 & 3 Class. a.m.	1 & 2 Class. p.m.	1 & 3 Class. p.m.	FARES FROM OXFORD.		
Miles.						1st Class.	2nd Class.	3rd Class.
	OXFORD .	9 0	11 50	5 40	8 30	s. d.	s. d.	s. d.
3½	YARNTON .	9 10	12 0	5 50	8 40	0 10	0 7	0 5
7	EYNSHAM .	9 18	12 8	5 57	8 48	1 8	1 2	0 10
9	SOUTH LEIGH .	9 25	12 15	6 5	8 55	2 1	1 5	1 0½
11½	WITNEY .	9 35	12 25	6 15	9 5	2 6	1 9	1 3

Worcester, November 8, 1861.

A. C. SHERRIFF,
GENERAL MANAGER.

was allocated to Oxford for Abingdon branch working from 1938 to 1947 and became the very last surviving '517' class engine, being withdrawn in August 1947. Another quite famous '517', No 1473 *Fair Rosamund*, well known as the Woodstock branch engine, was definitely working at Abingdon from September to December 1907. Another interesting locomotive to have worked the branch at the turn of the century was ex-Monmouthshire Railway No 1306, a 4-4-0T allocated to Oxford in 1900 and 1901 and withdrawn in 1904.

When Nationalisation came, the line was worked by 0-4-2T locomotives of the '1400' and '5800' classes until its closure to passengers in 1963. Latterly, until it closed down altogether in June 1984, a Class 08 diesel shunter provided the local trip working to the small coal yard.

The Witney Railway

As the large railway companies gradually extended their lines across the country, many small market towns sought to be connected to the main networks. One of these was Witney. During the 19th century Witney was an important centre for the wool trade and blanket making, and a railway would help to enhance this trade. It was to this end that in 1858 local tradesmen and mill owners promoted the Witney Railway Co. This would connect Witney to the nearby OW&WR line at Yarnton, a distance of some eight miles. An earlier proposal made by the OW&WR for a 4½ mile branch to Witney was never undertaken. The Act was duly passed in 1859 and work on the railway started at Eynsham in May 1860 and with little major engineering work being necessary was soon finished and ready to open on 14 November 1861.

The line left the OW&WR by way of a junction at Yarnton and ran via Cassington and Eynsham to a small one platform terminus station on the outskirts of Witney. The opening timetable shows departures from Witney to Oxford at 08.15am, 11.00am, 4.50pm and 7.35pm; with fares of 2s 6d first class, 1s 9d second and 1s 3d third.

A small single road engine shed was provided at Witney where the branch engine was stabled. This small shed closed in January 1873, when the line was extended to Fairford, the locomotives were then transferred to the new East Gloucestershire shed. The shed at Witney continued to be used for storage purposes for many years, eventually being demolished during November 1905.

Intermediate stations were provided at Eynsham and South Leigh; the line was soon to prove very successful and in 1862 a scheme to link Witney with Cheltenham was suggested. This proposal by the East Gloucestershire Railway Company was for an extension of the Faringdon Branch to Fairford and Cheltenham with a connecting link from Fairford to Witney, so putting Witney on a direct route from London to Cheltenham. However, as with many early schemes finances soon began to run out and the Cheltenham-Faringdon section was abandoned leaving the Witney-Fairford section the only stretch to be completed.

This second section of approximately 14 miles was duly opened for public service on 15 January 1873. Under an agreement which gave it a 50% share of the gross receipts the GWR operated the new section for the EGR Company. On the opening, the old terminus station at Witney ceased to be used except as a

goods yard and all traffic used a new station at Witney situated a short distance away on the new extension line. This station had two platforms, a booking office and waiting room and also a small signalbox situated on the up side. Initially intermediate stations were provided at Brize Norton and Bampton (Oxon). The terminus of the line was not at the single platformed Fairford station, but actually another ¼ mile westwards where a small engine shed and turntable stood, the line finishing at this point; still approximately ¾ mile from Fairford town itself.

Below:
Witney station looking towards Oxford.
Lens of Sutton

Bottom:
Almost at the end of the line, Fairford, terminus of the East Gloucestershire extension from Witney. 0-6-0PT No 7411 leaves with the afternoon train to Oxford. *Ian Allan Library*

The early EGR timetables show five trains per day each way, two of which were mixed; an additional train was run from Witney to Oxford and back on Thursday (market day) and one train each way on Sundays. Fairford shed had an allocation of two locomotives and four locomotive crews, being throughout its life a sub-depot of Oxford. The EGR continued to operate its foreshortened line to Fairford until the GWR took over the company on 1 July 1890. Had the line been built in its entirety, it would certainly have been an important through route. However, the completed second section from Witney to Fairford never really produced the expected revenue and only during World War 2 were the line's fortunes briefly revived. With the airfields of Fairford and Carterton being in close proximity to the line the passenger usage increased enormously and for this reason a new station was opened at Carterton during 1944. However, once the war had ended, the section from Witney to Fairford reverted to its prewar low usage. Fairford had always been served by a twice-daily goods from Oxford but traffic had dropped to such an extent that in the late 1950s one of these terminated at Witney, leaving only the early morning freight working though to the terminus.

Throughout its life Witney was the only really busy station on the branch, handling most of the traffic. In 1957 for example some 44,000 tons of goods and some 66,000 parcels left the station. It was only this traffic that sustained the line during its final years of operation. With the increase in road usage to distribute goods and parcels, together with the steady decline in the blanket industry during the early 1960s, passengers alone could not

justify the losses being incurred and it was no real surprise when the line closed to passenger traffic on 18 June 1962, with the original Witney-Yarnton section being retained for goods only. The last years before closure provided only four trains per day through to Fairford with no Saturday service. The East Gloucestershire extension line from Witney to Fairford was lifted during the autumn of 1964, and the original 1861 station at Witney once again became the terminus of the line. A systematic rundown of the remaining goods and coal traffic took place as more and more of this was diverted to the roads, until eventually in 1970 a decision was made to close the line completely and this was duly undertaken on 2 November 1970. Various special trains ran during the final months; the very last being a BR sponsored 'Witney Wanderer', a nine-car DMU, on 31 October 1970. The track was finally removed the following summer.

It is interesting to note that in October 1923 a proposal by local representatives and MPs was put to the GWR 'for the building of a new line some eight miles in length from Fairford to Cirencester, at an estimated cost of £321,000. This would connect with the ex-MSWJ Railway at Cirencester and provide a new shorter route to Cheltenham'. The GWR did not support the proposal, pointing out that a shortening of the route would lead to a general loss of revenue elsewhere, and the

extra employment that it would bring locally would be negligible, therefore concluding that they could not justify the building of this line. The government of the day accepted the objections and the connection was never constructed.

A notable feature of the branch was the installation in 1906 by the GWR of automatic train control: this was the first single line to be so equipped and such was its success that all of the distant signals from Yarnton Junction to Fairford were removed and replaced with ATC ramps.

Certainly the line saw some interesting motive power over the years and became the last haunt for many ancient locomotives. The two last examples of the 'Queen' class 2-2-2, Nos 1124 and 1128 were used until their subsequent withdrawals; No 1128 being the very last example, succumbing in April 1914. The last GWR 2-2-2 No 165 also worked on the branch until withdrawal in December 1914. Both Nos 165 and 1128 were fitted with ATC in 1906 in connection with experiments with this apparatus on the branch.

It is with the 'Metropolitan' 2-4-0 tanks that the branch will always be associated, as locomotives of this type provided much of the motive power on the line for some 50 years. In fact, when No 3588 was withdrawn from Fairford in December 1949 it was the very last example of this once numerous class.

The Wycombe Railway

On 1 August 1854 the Wycombe Railway Co had opened a broad gauge line from the Great Western main line at Maidenhead northwards to High Wycombe, the line was worked from the start by the GWR. In June 1861 powers were granted for the line to be extended to Thame and eventually to Oxford. The first part of this extension reached Thame in July 1862 and the line was opened after inspection on 1 August of that year. The first train carrying directors and shareholders arrived at 3pm that day, hauled by *Sunbeam*, a 'Sun' class 2-2-2 broad gauge engine designed in 1840 by Gooch. Regular passenger traffic started from Thame to Paddington on 2 August 1862.

The second part of the line from Thame to Kennington Junction, south of Oxford, was started by December 1862. This section of the line contained two major engineering works, a 1,584ft tunnel at Horsepath and a 270ft bridge

across the River Thames at Kennington. Both of these structures were completed during 1863. The new section was opened on 24 October 1864 and offered a second broad gauge route from Oxford to Paddington via Thame, Wycombe and Maidenhead. The broad gauge did not survive for long, however, as the line was closed on 23 August 1870, for gauge conversion, reopening as a standard gauge line on 1 September 1870. The next stage in the development of the route took place when the Great Central and Great Western joint line was opened from Wycombe to Marylebone and Paddington during 1906; from this date trains from Oxford to Paddington by way of Thame and Wycombe ran via this new route instead of the longer Bourne End and Maidenhead section. The new line, at 56 miles, was actually 7½ miles shorter than the regular Oxford-Reading route to Paddington. A particularly interesting working on the line during the 1950s was the 6.50pm Oxford-Paddington which still took the original 1864 Wycombe Railway route via Thame, Princes Risborough, Bourne End and Maidenhead. It was, however, only advertised to passengers as far as Risborough, thereafter becoming virtually a parcels train for the rest of its trip.

Left:
The turntable and rather overgrown yard at Yarnton. *R. H. G. Simpson*

Below:
Littlemore station at the turn of the century. To the right stands the county lunatic asylum.
L&GRP (8492)

Left:

Wheatley station in the 1920s. Note the cattle wagons in the up bay. To the right stands Avery's sawmill with a steam traction engine in the yard. *L&GRP (8529)*

Below:

Timetable of GWR steam railmotor service. *Author's collection*

OXFORD & PRINCES RISBOROUGH.

WEEK DAYS.

		a.m.	a.m.	M a.m	a.m.	p.m.		Mxd p.m.	M p.m.	p.m.	p.m.		M p.m.	M
OXFORD	dep.	7 10	8 26	10 25	11 20	1 6		2 28	4 50	6 25			8 50	
Hinksey Halt	,,			10 29		1 9			4 54	...			8 54	
Abingdon Road Halt	,,			10 31		1 10			4 57				8 56	
Iffley Halt	,,			10 34		1 14			5 0	...			8 59	
Littlemore	,,	7 20	8 37	10 38	11 29	1 17		2 40	5 4	6 34			9 3	
Garsington Bridge Halt	,,			10 42		1 20			5 8	...			9 7	
Horsepath Halt	,,			10 46		1 24			5 12				9 11	
Wheatley	,,	7 30	8 47	10 51	11 39	1 31		2 50	5 19	6 46			9 17	
Tiddington	,,	7 39	8 55		11 46	1 40		2 57	5 28	6 57			9 26	
Thame	,,	7 48	9 10		11 57	1 51		3 7	4 30	5 39	7 9		9 36	9 38
Bledlow	,,	7 57	9 22		12 7	2 2		3 16	4 40	5 50	7 18			9 49
Princes Risborough	arr.	8 2	9 28		12 12	2 7		3 21	4 48	5 55	7 25			9 54

		a.m.	a.m.	M a.m.	a.m.	p.m		M p.m.	p.m.	p.m.	M p.m.	p.m.		M p.m.
Princes Risborough	dep.	8 8	9 31	...	11 6		12 54	2 13	3 55	6 33	7 33			10 20
Bledlow	,,	8 13	9 36	...	11 11		1 0	2 18	4 1	6 39	7 38			10 25
Thame	,,	8 24	9 46	...	11 18		1 11	2 30	4 12	7 *10	7 47	9 45		10 37
Tiddington	,,	8 32	9 57	...			1 20	2 41	4 23	7 21	7 55	9 56		10 48
Wheatley	,,	8 47	10 6	11 3			1 30	3 ¶ 3	4 31	7 31	8 3	10 6		10 58
Horsepath Halt	,,			11 9				3 9		7 37		10 12		11 4
Garsington Bridge Halt	,,			11 13				3 13		7 41		10 16		11 8
Littlemore	,,	8 57	10 16	11 18			1 40	3 17	4 40	7 45	8 12	10 20		11 12
Iffley Halt	,,			11 21				3 20		7 48		10 23		11 15
Abingdon Road Halt	,,			11 29		12 19		3 24		7 51		10 26		11 18
Hinksey Halt	,,			11 32		12 21		3 26		7 53		10 28		11 20
OXFORD	arr.	9 5	10 25	11 38		12 25		1 52	3 30	4 47	7 57	8 20	10 32		11 25

M Rail Motor Car, one class only. * Arrive Thame 6.50 p.m. ¶ Arrive Wheatley 2.49 p.m.

Because of considerable subsidence, the river bridge at Kennington was replaced in 1923 by a completely new girder bridge built alongside the original one; on completion the old 1863 bridge was removed. The brick abutments of the old bridge still remain today.

The route from Kennington Junction to Princes Risborough was a single line with crossing points at the two principal stations, Wheatley and Thame. Wheatley station was provided with both up and down platforms, the modest station buildings were situated on the up side, together with several sidings, and a small signalbox. Thame station by comparison was a much grander affair, with a superb Brunel-style train shed; this timber structure measured some 46ft wide by 90ft long. It survived intact until the line was closed to passengers in 1963. Thame also had extensive sidings, together with a large goods shed. A 28-lever signalbox stood opposite this shed on the down side. Intermediate stations were provided at Littlemore, Tiddington, and Bedlow. In 1908, the arrival of steam railmotors at Oxford allowed additional halts to be provided on the main line at Hinksey and

Abingdon Road, and on the branch at Iffley, Garsington Road bridge, and Horspath. These were all closed during 1915, when the railmotors left the area.

When the Morris Motor works together with the Pressed Steel Co opened their respective factories at Cowley in the 1920s, the line attained additional importance as a means of providing freight traffic to and from these two large works. A station was provided at Cowley during 1928 on the site of the old Garsington Bridge halt and named, appropriately, Morris Cowley after William Morris, the founder of

Morris Motors Ltd. Extensive sidings, together with a signalbox were also provided at this time. In 1933 a new halt was built at Horspath on the site of the earlier 1908 railmotor platform.

Apart from the everyday branch trains, the line was regularly used as a diversionary route during engineering works on the Paddington-Birmingham via Bicester main line. Wheatley

Right:
Class '9F' 2-10-0 No 92220 *Evening Star* carrying an 81F (Oxford) shedplate leaves Morris Cowley on 2 March 1963 with the 1.50pm Bathgate car train. *J. Hubbard*

Below:
'6100' class 2-6-2T No 6106 stands alongside the signalbox at Morris Cowley. In the background can be seen two small Fowler 0-4-0 diesel locomotives owned by the Pressed Steel Co for working within the factory complex. *J. D. Edwards*

Left:

Today the railhead at Cowley still sees much car traffic, as it did in 1959 when this picture was taken. Here 2-6-0 No 6326 leaves the branch at Kennington Junction en route to the Scottish Motor Show with a train load of BMC cars and parts on 6 November 1959. *J. D. Edwards*

Below left:

The driver of 2-8-0 No 3857 waits with the tablet as he approaches Kennington Junction box with a freight off the branch from Morris Cowley yard on 3 September 1959. *J. D. Edwards*

Above right:

'5100' class 2-6-2T No 4148 takes the branch at Kennington Junction with the 2.51pm train to Princes Risborough on 26 August 1961. The single line token apparatus can be seen to the right of the locomotive. *A. Simpkins*

Right:

0-4-2T No 1444 stands inside the BMC works at Cowley in 1961. This locomotive was on hire to BMC at the time when their own diesel locomotive was being repaired. The figure in the foreground is local railwayman 'Cheddar' Wilson. *D. Pye*

also saw many extra trains during World War 2 when a military hospital was built at nearby Holton. Regular hospital trains ran usually from the Oxford direction up to Wheatley station to transfer the wounded to the hospital. Local inhabitants clearly remember the convoys of army ambulances from Wheatley station to the Holton Park Hospital.

Under the Beeching cuts of the early 1960s the line saw its last scheduled passenger train on 6 January 1963. The line continued to operate with much parcels and goods traffic but the poor state of Horspath tunnel and the high cost of repair (approximately £60,000) ensured the closure of the line as a through route. The centre section from Horspath to Thame was closed to all traffic in 1965 and the track on this section lifted, thereby cutting the line effectively into two separate branches. The line from Risborough to Thame is still open for oil traffic to a terminal situated near the remains of Thame Station. At the Oxford end the line remains open to Cowley, serving on the way a BP oil terminal siding at Littlemore that can accommodate up to 12 32-tonne wagons and has one to four deliveries per week according to seasonal demand.

The railhead at Morris Cowley now sees much traffic; the nearby car works being a large customer. Three car trains leave Cowley each day carrying many vehicles both for the home and export markets. These are the 16.20 to Bescot, 20.00 to Parkeston Quay and the 21.00 to Bathgate; in 1984 over 50,000 vehicles were carried in this way. The general goods traffic is handled at the nearby International Freight Terminal and during May 1985 the second phase of the joint BR/F. C. Bennetts' project was completed at a cost of approximately £370,000. A 20,000sq ft warehouse now handles such diverse items as wines and spirits, aluminium ingots, newsprint and fertilizer, via the British Rail Speedlink service. Certainly, with all this increased usage the remains of the Wycombe Railway, in the Oxford area, will continue to survive for many years to come.

Motive Power

Over the years passenger trains on the branch were always worked by small tank engines; Victorian days saw many services in the hands of 'Metro' and '517' class engines with 'Armstrong Standard' and 'Dean Goods' 0-6-0 locomotives forming the mainstay of the freight traffic on the line. The early part of the 20th century (as already mentioned) brought the steam railmotors to the branch, but these did not survive for long.

The 1920s and early 1930s saw 'Bulldog' and 'County' class 4-4-0s working on the branch but these soon left, leaving many of the services in the hands of the newly constructed '6100' class 2-6-2Ts, which were to provide motive power on the line right through to closure. From 1935 the GW introduced some of the new diesel railcars on to the line and these continued to supplement the services until they were withdrawn from the area in 1957.

The line's importance as a diversionary route from London to Birmingham brought many of the larger passenger classes of GWR engines on to the line; over the years examples of 'Castles', 'Granges', 'Halls', 'Saints' and 'Stars' all made regular appearances. From 1960, many of the car trains from Morris Cowley saw regular haulage by the large BR 'Standard' class engines, with the Bathgate train producing 'Britannia' Pacifics, as well as '9F' 2-10-0 locomotives and '75000' class 4-6-0s on the Birmingham working.

Even in 1986, the present terminus of the Oxford end at Morris Cowley produces a good selection of diesels, with the local trip in the hands of Classes 31 and 47. The 16.20 Bescot train has produced Classes 20, 25, 31, 45, 47, 56 and 58 whilst the 20.00 Parkeston Quay service regularly utilises a Class 50 locomotive.

Blenheim for Woodstock

This was the last local branch line to open. It ran for 3¾ miles from the Great Western Railway Oxford-Birmingham main line at Kidlington to a small terminus station situated near the centre of Woodstock. This railway must have been rather unique, since for the whole of its working life the terminus was known as Blenheim for Woodstock, taking the name of the nearby stately home of the Duke of Marlborough. The then Duke had provided most of the capital required for the building of the Woodstock Railway and so, when it was opened to the public on 19 May 1890, the station sign together with the timetables announced the name of the palace first, and it was as this that the line was to be known for the whole of its working life.

The line left a bay platform on the down side of the main Oxford-Birmingham line at Kidlington station, which had been named Woodstock Road until the opening of the branch, it then ran northwards parallel to the main line for approximately 1 mile, before branching away to cross both the Oxford Canal and the River Cherwell in quick succession before also crossing the main A423 Oxford-Banbury road. It was at this latter point that the only intermediate station on the branch was situated. Shipton-on-Cherwell halt was opened in April 1929, with its single wooden platform and small shelter positioned on the north side of the branch on the Woodstock side of the road bridge. The line continued for a

further 1½ miles to the small town of
Woodstock, where it terminated alongside the
A34 road adjacent to the main entrance to
Blenheim Palace.

The line was worked from the start by the
GWR and was eventually sold by the
Woodstock Railway to this company in 1897
for £15,000. Throughout the life of the branch,
with few fluctuations, Woodstock was served
by eight trains per day, with one morning and
one afternoon train travelling through to
Oxford.

With such a close proximity to Oxford, the
bus and car ensured dwindling receipts for
both passenger and freight traffic. It was no
real surprise when the line closed completely.

Below:

The first local branch line to close was the Woodstock branch as the closure notice seen here advises. *OURS collection*

The last train was the 6.48pm to Oxford hauled by 0-4-2T No 1420 on Saturday 27 February 1954, the line being officially closed on Monday 1 March. This was the first local branch to go. Little now remains of the branch; Kidlington station on the main line has gone but the old terminus building at Woodstock is still in use, as a garage.

The branch was always worked by small tank engines which were serviced at the engine shed situated in the goods yard at Woodstock. For many years one engine was allocated here to work the branch but the shed closed in 1927 and thereafter the branch locomotive was serviced at Oxford. Early workings were by GWR '517' class 0-4-2T locomotives and in later years by their successors the '4800' class 0-4-2 tanks, with the occasional 0-6-0 pannier tank. It is with one of the '517' class that the Woodstock branch will always be associated, the locomotive being No 1473 built at Wolverhampton in 1883, and which on the occasion that it worked a Royal Train on the branch in 1896 was given the name *Fair Rosamund*. This locomotive continued to work regularly on the branch until it was withdrawn in August 1935, some 39 years later. The name derived, rather interestingly, from the Lady Rosamund who lived at Blenheim Palace and was the mistress of Henry VIII.

Below:

Saturday 27 February 1954 and 0-4-2T No 1420 leaves the bay at Kidlington for the last time, on its journey to Woodstock. The 6.48pm was the very last service train on the Woodstock branch, as the branch closed completely from Monday 1 March 1954. *G. Hine*

The London & North Western Railway at Oxford

The Buckinghamshire Railway terminus at Rewley Road opened on 20 May 1851. The station was unique as it was built in the style of the Crystal Palace by the firm Fox, Henderson Ltd, using the same Paxton designed method of construction. This utilised prefabricated cast iron, bolt together sections — a pioneer method of unit building at that time.

The station was provided with an island platform covered by a large glass roofed train shed. At the terminus end stood the station frontage which contained the entrance hall and office accommodation. Up to 1888 the overall roof was glazed longitudinally but was extensively rebuilt at this date with the glazing panels running laterally across the roof in a standard Northlight pattern. With the withdrawal of the low six-wheeled coaches from the branch in 1909, the 450ft long wooden platform was raised to the standard height of 36in and paved. Trains would usually arrive at Platform 2 but would very often leave from either platform. From 1880 the station was provided with a circular booking office which also doubled as the Stationmaster's office. This structure is said to have been used at the Great Exhibition of 1851, but was sadly broken up shortly after the station closed in 1951.

The complete station structure survived almost intact until closure, although much of the roof glazing was in an advanced state of decay. For a number of years after closure, the building was used as a railway hostel, but this also ceased in the late 1960s when the building was taken over by a local tyre company who are still there in 1986.

During this time the platform and train shed have been removed, leaving only the main building, booking hall and canopy, of which the metal framework is a listed structure. The former goods yard and station area is now closed and the site has been completely cleared in anticipation of redevelopment. If this takes place it is planned to use the remaining metal framework of this elegant station to form a new entrance to the proposed new Western Region station at Oxford.

Passenger services from Rewley Road to Bletchley were always of a semi-fast nature, with most trains stopping at each of the eight intermediate stations. This gave an average journey time of about 63min. Early timetables show a service of six trains per day in each direction and by the turn of the century this had increased to eight, and now included a through service to Bedford and Cambridge. Most of these services also connected at Bletchley with trains to and from London.

The line always carried much excursion traffic and it was on some of these that the fastest running on the line was achieved. In 1934 a Colne-Oxford excursion hauled by Deeley Compound 4-4-0 No 1102 with a load of seven coaches attained an average speed of 52mph for the 27¾ miles between Bletchley and Oxford Road Junction. Service trains have also 'moved' when required, and with such an easy schedule for the 31½-mile route, early

Right:
The London & North Western Railway office in Cornmarket Street, Oxford, adjacent to the Clarendon Hotel stable entrance; seen c1875. The same spot 110 years later provides the entrance to the new Clarendon Shopping Centre.
Minn collection Bodleian Library

Top:
The LNWR 'Precursor' class 4-4-0 locomotives provided the motive power on the Bletchley-Oxford trains for many years before and after World War 1. This picture taken in July 1930 shows one of these fine engines, No 5246 *Adjutant* waiting at Rewley Road, Oxford, with an afternoon train to Bletchley. *OURS collection*

Above:
The interior of the ex-LNWR Rewley Road station. *National Railway Museum*

Above right:
The ex-LNWR Rewley Road station at Oxford, seen during the early 1940s in LMS hands. Note the amount of coal traffic in the yard. *National Railway Museum*

Right:
An ex-LNWR 0-6-2T No 7733 stands partially on the swing bridge over the Sheepwash Channel at the entrance to Rewley Road yard in April 1930. *OURS collection*

arrivals were quite a regular occurrence.

The line saw a marked increase in traffic, with the opening of Bicester Ordnance Depot and Oxford North Junction in 1940. The passenger traffic on the line increased considerably at this time with many service personnel travelling to and from Bicester. A regular feature of wartime Oxford was the running of the 'Saturday Night Specials' from the Ordnance Depot Railway to Oxford, hauled usually by either a couple of War Department 'Dean Goods' 0-6-0s or an old ex-LSWR Adams 'Jubilee' 0-4-2, No 625.

After the war the GWR, who now had control of the line as far as Bicester, continued to run a

Below left:
Oxford North Junction, ex-Midland '3F' 0-6-0 No 43785 leaves on the 5.18pm train from Oxford to Bedford on 8 September 1954. By this date the ex-LNWR station at Oxford was closed and trains for Bedford and Cambridge left from the down bay platform at the ex-Great Western Railway station. *Dr G. D. Parkes*

Below:
Tickets to and from Rewley Road.
OURS collection

morning passenger train, the 10.50am from Oxford right into the WD railway as far as Piddington. This service continued up until the late 1950s. The year 1951 saw the ex-LNWR station close to passenger traffic and from October of that year passengers travelling to and from Bletchley left from the adjacent Western Region station, trains using the up or down bay platforms via Oxford North Junction. The frequency had now increased to 10 trains per day with two through afternoon services to Bedford and Cambridge via the 2.28pm and the 5.15pm.

Talk of closure came in the early 1960s but a partial reprieve came with the use of the two-car DMUs on the line, surprisingly using

Left:

No 25802, an ex-LNWR 'Prince of Wales' class 4-6-0 built in 1915, stands on the small turntable at the former LNWR loco depot at Oxford, having just worked in from Bletchley. The local landmark of St Barnabas church in Jericho stands on the left in the background.
R. H. G. Simpson

Above:

Stanier 2-6-4T No 42667 leaves Oxford Rewley Road on 1 October 1951 with the very last passenger working from this station, the 4.45pm to Bletchley. After this date all passenger trains to and from Bletchley used either the up or down bays at the adjacent ex-GWR station. *R. Bowen*

the same steam schedule of about 63min. Closure did come, however, and the last passenger service left Oxford at 22.50 on 30 December 1967. Since the closure there has been much talk of reopening the line for passenger traffic, possibly running as far as the New City of Milton Keynes. Who knows, perhaps in a few years' time we may once again be able to travel on the Buckinghamshire Railway.

There has always been a great deal of goods and freight carried on the LNWR line from Oxford to Bletchley and beyond, and certainly during the 19th and 20th centuries much of Oxford's domestic coal arrived at Rewley Road for subsequent distribution. With the rather small transfer connection at Oxford between the LNWR and the GWR, a certain amount of interchange of freight traffic took place, but it was not until the junction was built at Oxford North in 1940 that this traffic increased. Such was this increase that sidings were put in at Port Meadow allowing trains requiring access to the GWR main line to wait, in order not to block the busy passenger lines. The peak period for usage had been during World War 2, but even after hostilities ceased a considerable amount of traffic was still using this junction, with trains running from Swanbourne Yard to Hinksey.

With the many brickworks that were situated alongside the route between Calvert

and Bedford, brick trains always formed an important part of the freight working. These trains ran regularly from the various works via the Yarnton loop to westward destinations. The subsequent switch from rail to road for this traffic during the 1950s, together with the demise of many of the brickworks, saw the disappearance of these workings. During World War 2 the yard at Yarnton was enlarged and a turntable installed, which allowed East-West traffic to travel via the loop and exchange sidings at Yarnton. The turntable was large enough to take the biggest engines and in the 1950s and 1960s, Standard '9Fs' became frequent visitors. One interesting working was the 7.10pm Ipswich-Cardiff express freight which ran via Cambridge, Bletchley and Yarnton. This train regularly used Eastern Region locomotives to Yarnton, including 'B1s', 'K3s' and 'J39s'. In 1962, the flyover at Bletchley opened, the intention being to run many more of the cross-country freights. However, a subsequent change of policy meant that this was little used and when the Bedford to Sandy line was closed in 1968, the flyover became a £1.6 million white

elephant. The Yarnton loop itself had been closed during 1965. In 1973 the wartime junction at Oxford North was removed and a new junction was installed near Aristotle Lane, about half a mile further to the north. At this time the line from Oxford to Bicester was singled. Today the line is still busy with the Stoke Gifford-Wolverton stone trains, the Bath-Calvert refuse train and the daily local trips to Bicester Central Ordnance Depot; regular parcels trains also use this route. The manual signalbox at Bicester West was due to close on 24 May 1986, with the line singled to Claydon LNER junction. With single line working the line will then have the capacity of about 18 trains per day. Some of the disused brick quarries along the line are scheduled to receive compacted waste from London, making additional use of the line to that already mentioned.

Motive power on freight traffic into Oxford on this line during the 1950s and 1960s produced many LMS '8F' 2-8-0s but the ex-LNWR 'G1' and 'G2' 0-8-0 engines were always regular visitors, coming mostly from Bletchley and Nuneaton sheds. The 1950s saw

Above:
Above:
This superb panorama formed of two separate photographs shows the ex-LNWR station and yard at Oxford, which by this time was closed to passengers. The GWR station stands to the left, together with the wooden steam depot (centre background). *J. D. Edwards*

the arrival of Standard locomotives on the line and Class 4 4-6-0s together with '9F' 2-10-0s took over most of the freight turns, the '9Fs' coming in from both Wellingborough and Toton depots. 1965 saw the last steam workings on the line with the closure of both Bletchley and Oxford depots in that year.

The Great Western Railway was not alone in providing locomotive servicing facilities at Oxford, for in 1851 the LNWR had built a small locomotive shed alongside its line from Bletchley, just a few hundred yards north of the Rewley Road terminus station. This small three road through shed was constructed of corrugated iron and contained quite a large workshop along its eastern side. Room was provided for up to nine locomotives, quite a large number, for in 1855 it was reported that

daily on the branch there were five locomotives in steam with two in reserve. The small yard contained a 42ft turntable and a large 16,000gal water tower, both standing to the south side of the shed structure. The water was pumped to the tower, via a steam pump, from the River Thames which ran alongside the shed. This shed was always a sub-depot of Bletchley and was given the code 4 by the LNWR in 1874, being changed some years later to 30. The shed continued to fulfil its purpose but generally suffered from decay, and it was no great surprise when, on 14 October 1877, severe gales in the area demolished a substantial part of the shed roof. This was subsequently repaired but on 15 June 1879 the workshop and part of the shed were damaged by a small fire: again, repairs were undertaken but the structure was by now in a poor state. It was not long before the LNWR made the decision to demolish the old depot, and provide Oxford with a more substantial structure. This work was undertaken in the early part of 1883, and soon a brick-built standard Webb Northlight pattern, two-road shed some 150ft in length was erected on the site of the old shed. This

Above:
The swing bridge at the entrance to Rewley Road in 1985. This bridge is to be restored to its original condition as a static exhibit; since this picture was taken all trackwork has been removed from the yard. *Author*

new building was slightly smaller than the original structure, having space inside for only six locomotives. It was not a through shed however, the offices and workshop being situated at the north end. The original water tower and turntable were retained. The estimated cost of replacing the old depot was recorded as £1,817.

The depot remained little altered until 1928, when a new 50ft diameter turntable was provided in place of the previous 42ft example, thus allowing larger locomotives to use the branch. The coaling of locomotives was always a primitive affair at this shed, undertaken by hand, outside and from open wagons with no cover provided. It was not until March 1950 that cover was provided for the coaling area; this was a rather pointless exercise as the shed closed on 3 December 1950, and the shed staff of 20-30 men was transferred to the ex-GWR depot opposite. The empty shed and water tower stood unused for some years, the water tower was removed in 1960 followed by the brick shed structure in early 1962.

Many interesting types of locomotive have used the servicing facilities at this small depot after working in from Bletchley and beyond. Early this century most of the trains were in

Above right:
Rewley Road signalbox in the ex-LNWR yard at Oxford. The famous swing bridge is situated just a few yards to the north of the box; the rodding for points and signal wiring can be seen on the raised construction alongside the bridge. Oxford Station North box stands in the background. Note the GWR fire buckets on the box balcony. *J. D. Edwards*

Right:
The remains of the ex-LNWR shed at Rewley Road in 1959. *J. D. Edwards*

Below:

A Bowen Cooke LNWR 'Prince of Wales' Class 4-6-0 No 25673 *Lusitania* **stands alongside the water tower at the LNWR shed in Oxford. These engines were regular visitors to Oxford over the years. When this picture was taken on 2 March 1947,** *Lusitania* **only had a few more months of working before withdrawal.** *R. G. H. Simpson*

Bottom:

The remains of the LNWR terminus at Oxford are today a tyre depot. The historic girder structure can be seen to good effect in this picture, taken in May 1985. *Author*

the hands of 'Lady of the Lake' class 2-2-2 locomotives with Webb 0-6-2 tank engines supplementing the service, the latter continuing on the line until the 1940s. Other locomotives over the years included members of the 'Precursor', 'Precedent' and 'Prince of Wales' classes. In fact, the last surviving 'Prince of Wales' No 25845, a 4-6-0 built in 1915, worked regularly on the branch until it was withdrawn in November 1947. Some of the last locomotives to use the depot facilities were LMS 'Jinty' 0-6-0Ts, Johnson 4-4-0 Type '3s' and LMS '8F' 2-8-0 locomotives. During the war years regular visitors to the depot on workings from Bicester Military Railway were two ex-GWR 'Dean Goods' 0-6-0 and an ex-Southern Railway Adams 0-4-2. These were operated by the WD at this time.

Today the site is completely overgrown and it is almost impossible to imagine the impressive structure which stood on this site for some 78 years.

The Great Western Station

When the Great Western Railway opened its line from Millstream Junction in 1850 northwards to Birmingham and beyond, the increase in traffic that resulted during ensuing years meant that the new station opened by the company at Oxford in 1852 to replace the earlier broad gauge station at Grandpont, was rapidly becoming hopelessly inadequate both in size and facilities to provide for the increase in passenger and goods traffic generated.

To reduce this problem the station and adjacent area were subject to continuous improvements between the years 1879 and 1910. The initial station provided by the GWR in 1852 for Oxford comprised a Brunel-designed overall roof with two short platforms, the down platform being slightly longer than the up platform. It also contained a bay at the north end, used by the OW&WR line trains, which from June 1853 had running rights into Oxford. Small waiting rooms were provided on each platform for 1st and 2nd class travellers only. Public toilet facilities were provided on the up side only, and these soon proved to be totally inadequate and generated much complaint from passengers and staff alike. As a result, the staff toilets on the down side were given over to passenger use from 1864.

The first alteration to the station came in 1872 when the broad gauge was removed. The extra room within the track bed allowed the up and down platforms to be widened by several feet and this was duly completed by August 1874. The old broad gauge engine shed at the north end of the station yard was used as a carriage shed from 1872 and was removed in 1879 allowing further improvements to be made to the yard. The entrance to this remodelled yard was effected by a new junction constructed some 50yd to the north, the old backshunt at the end of the up platform was also removed at this time, and this certainly eased congestion somewhat at this point. These minor alterations did nothing, however, to improve the general facilities for passengers and it was no great surprise when the GWR announced in the *Oxford Journal* of October 1890, the following:

'The Great Western Railway at Oxford: The directors of this Company have authorised the expenditure of nearly £10,000 for the purpose of providing better accommodation at Oxford Station and the contract for the greater part of it was let early last month to Mr Samuel Robertson, Contractor of Bristol.'

This work comprised removing the large circular span overall roof, together with the square wooden columns supporting it; these being replaced by iron columns and a small span glass roof running along each platform. New waiting rooms were built on both platforms for 1st, 2nd and 3rd class accommodation and, more important, new larger toilets were provided on both up and down platforms; these toilets 'being now based on the latest scientific principles' (this probably means that they were flush toilets). The up platform was also extended by about 110ft northward, and the down platform roof covering was extended by about 140ft; new parcels offices were provided on both the up and down platforms. The subway beneath these two platforms was also improved. This major remodelling of the station was started almost immediately. The overall roof was removed in November 1890

Below:
The GWR station at Oxford circa 1919.
L&GRP (11939)

47

and the remainder of the remodelling work was finished by October 1891.

Oxford now had a station more in keeping with the increased passenger and goods usage of the 1890s and for a while this proved to be quite adequate. It was the Great Central Railway's extension to Banbury Junction in 1900, and the increased traffic that this line generated on to an already busy GWR route, together with the increasing length of the trains, which prompted the GWR once again to alter the layout at Oxford. Both up and down platforms were still quite short; the down platform contained a small wagon turntable at

the south end. In 1907 the GWR decided to remove this and extend the down platform at both ends. This was completed in 1908 and left Oxford with a 918ft up and 916ft down platform. The up arrival bay was now 440ft long with the down departure bay 450ft long, at the same time the river bridge north of the station was enlarged to accommodate these new bay connections. To facilitate the running of two trains at a time into the main platforms, scissors crossovers were installed half-way along each platform line, connecting to the through up and down lines. The track on either side of these crossovers was only capable of handling a locomotive and five carriages, and with increased train lengths these crossovers were to be little used from the start. The last major alterations were made in 1910, when the uncovered section of the up platform was provided with a canopy for the majority of its

length. In this guise Oxford station remained little altered for the next 60 years until it was demolished in 1970 and replaced with the prefabricated structure that we can see today. Apart from the platforms themselves the only features remaining from the old station are the girders from the 1910 roof extension on the up platform; these provide the support for the canopy on the up side north end today.

Top:
The authorities were very sensitive regarding smoke pollution in the Oxford area, and to this effect notices regarding the excess emission of smoke were displayed on both up and down platform ends. This photograph depicts such a notice on the London end of the up platform. '7200' class 2-8-2T No 7239 stands in the up through road. *Author's collection*

Above:
This interesting picture, taken on Sunday 11 September 1960, shows double chimney fitted 'Castle' class locomotive No 5071 *Spitfire* of Worcester depot in the Cripley Road sidings at the north end of the station, waiting to form the 6.55pm to Wolverhampton. These sidings are now lifted and the site provides a new access road for motor vehicles to the diesel stabling point and offices. *M. Mensing*

Above:
Oxford down platform looking north c1964.
Author's collection

Below:
**The Botley Road bridge in 1958. Note the tight fit
even for this lowbridge AEC Regent III of City of
Oxford Motor Services.** *J. D. Edwards*

Top left:
Just occasionally a high-deck bus would find itself on the Botley route with the obvious catastrophic effect. Here highbridge AEC No 820 has suffered the ultimate indignity of losing its roof to the railway bridge. *R. G. Simpson*

Centre left:
Old and new platform ticket machines at Oxford up platform in 1958. The letters GWR can still be seen clearly on the right-hand machine; both, as was usual, are empty! *J. D. Edwards*

Facing page, bottom left:
Oxford up side ticket office in 1968.
Author's collection

Facing page, top right:
1969 and the by now rather dilapidated station awaits demolition. This picture shows the gas lighting that was still being used at this date.
Author's collection

Facing page, bottom right:
The up side entrance to Oxford in 1968.
Author's collection

Above:
This panorama shows the approaches to Oxford Western Region station in 1958. The notorious Botley Road bridge is to the left. The entrance to the subway, known locally as the 'Black Hole', is in the centre of the scene. *J. D. Edwards*

Centre right:
This picture taken during 1954 clearly shows the 1908 platform and roof extension to the up side of Oxford station; the scissors crossings can also be seen. The up bay holds the 9.15am ex-Fairford whilst in the up platform the 10.35am to Didcot awaits the connecting 9.27am from Bletchley.
OURS collection

Right:
Oxford station down side exterior looking southwards in July 1964; its clean and tidy appearance belies the advanced state of decay of most of its wooden structure. It was very soon after this date that a decision was made to rebuild the station completely.
Author's collection

Above and Above right:
The above two views illustrate the changing railway scene. First picture taken in 1960 shows the view from the north end of the down platform. Above right is the same view in 1985. *Author*

Right:
The second rebuilding of Oxford station took place in 1970. This picture taken during October of that year shows the partially demolished up platform. When the temporary footbridge was provided during subway rebuilding, it was to be the only occasion when the Oxford public could officially cross over the tracks. *John H. Bird*

Plans have for some time existed to replace the present station with a new one incorporating a large office block. The ex-LNWR yard and station site at Rewley Road will, at the same time, be redeveloped commercially. It is possible that the historic girder structure of the old LNWR station may be incorporated into the new forecourt.

Unfortunately the station is situated in an area of acute road traffic congestion and any redevelopment must be balanced against the possible increase in traffic generated. To this end a new Parkway station has been proposed;

Above:
In 1979 the Botley Road bridge was raised and much rail traffic through Oxford was suspended at weekends for the duration of the engineering work. Here two cranes prepare to remove one of the old cross-beams. *B. Higgins*

to be built on the site of the Hinksey marshalling yard south of Oxford. This yard built in 1940 is almost unused today. It is hoped that, by reducing the amount of vehicular traffic to the Central station, development work will be allowed on the site. If Oxford Parkway station is ever built it will, ironically, only be a stone's throw away from the site of the original 1844 terminus of the Oxford Railway.

Signalling at Oxford

When the Oxford Railway opened in June 1844 it is probable that little if any signalling was provided on the line, and that which there was would certainly have been of a very primitive nature. Even when the Great Western extended its route to Birmingham between 1850 and 1852, it was still using very basic methods of train control, with again probably few signals on the route. First evidence of the existence of signalboxes, locally, appears on the 1871 Ordnance Survey maps of the area, which

Top left:
'7400' class 0-6-0PT No 7445 passing Wolvercot siding signalbox circa 1958. This opened in 1900 and replaced an earlier box that once stood on this site. It was closed in June 1958, together with the loading platform that can be seen to the left of the picture. For many years this small platform had been used for the delivery of paper pulp to the nearby paper mill. *J. D. Edwards*

Centre left:
The metal signal gantry erected in 1959 at the north end of the station to replace early wooden signals is shown to great effect in this picture. Here '5100' class 2-6-2T No 5152 of Banbury depot hauls a mixed freight through the station to Hinksey yard. *A. Simpkins*

Bottom left:
The signalbox diagram together with some instruments at Oxford Station North box. This diagram is now safely kept by the Oxford Museum Services and will shortly be put on view. Station North closed together with the other manual boxes on 13 October 1973 when the new electric panel box was opened. *B. Higgins*

Right:
The unique Western Region upper quadrant signal, installed during 1950, was the Oxford North Junction up main starter. Removed during the conversion to MAS in the Oxford area during 1973, it now stands in the National Railway Museum at York. The train is the 3.25pm Banbury-Oxford hauled by 'Hall' 4-6-0 No 4985 *Allesley Hall* on 27 April 1959. *J. D. Edwards*

show boxes at Kennington Junction, Oxford station and Wolvercot Junction.

The LNWR line into Oxford Rewley Road at this time was controlled locally by two boxes, one at the Rewley Road terminus itself and another on the outskirts of Oxford at Oxford Road Junction. These two boxes, together with a third at Port Meadow which was opened during World War 2, provided signalling control on this line right up until both Rewley Road and Port Meadow boxes were closed in 1959 and 1960 respectively.

The GWR, however, continued to expand its lines and yards locally and by the turn of the century, signalboxes were situated at Culham, Nuneham, Radley, Kennington Junction, Oxford South, Oxford Goods, Oxford Engine Shed, Oxford North, Wolvercot Siding and Wolvercot Junction. The original Engine Shed box was situated at the north end of the station, in the small up yard. It was removed during the up platform extension work in 1908 and replaced by a completely new signalbox just a few yards north of the river bridge, again named Engine Shed box; this contained 97 levers and was the largest in the area.

Few changes took place in signalling at Oxford until the onset of World War 2, when in 1940 a new connection to the LNWR was provided at Oxford North. The box at this point was rebuilt and renamed Oxford North Junction. A new marshalling yard was constructed at Hinksey during 1942, and many additional sidings and loops were placed between Wolvercot Junction and Radley. To supplement these, new boxes were opened at Sandford during 1940 and at Hinksey North and South in 1942. In the latter year the box at Oxford South was closed and Oxford Goods and Engine Shed boxes were renamed Oxford Station South and Station North respectively. This now meant that the 6½ miles between Radley and Wolvercot Junction was controlled by no fewer than 10 signalboxes, many of which were open 24 hours per day.

In 1950 the Western Region replaced the ex-GW wooden up starter at Oxford North Junction with an experimental upper quadrant signal, the only one to remain in regular use on the whole of the Western Region. This unique signal continued to be used until it was removed in 1973. It is now on display at the National Railway Museum, York. In 1959 the Western Region replaced all the remaining wooden signals locally with standard steel types. Many were placed on new metal gantries, the largest of which stood at the north end of Oxford station, straddling the whole of the track layout at this point.

The end of semaphore signalling at Oxford came on 18 October 1973 when the new Oxford MAS power box was opened. On this date all

the remaining manual boxes in the area were closed. This small power box which is situated on the down platform at Oxford now controls the 26½ miles between Didcot North Junction and Heyford, as well as 13½ miles of the Cotswold Line as far as Ascott-under-Wychwood. It also controls the three miles to Morris Cowley freight terminal, and five miles from Oxford New North Junction to Islip. The only

reminder of the semaphore era at Oxford today is the old gantry at the south end of the up platform which is still used to carry the station up starter, albeit a Multiple Aspect type.

The nearest traditional manual signalbox to Oxford in use today is Appleford Crossing box, north of Didcot North Junction.

Below:
Oxford North Junction signalbox, built during 1940 by Italian prisoners of war. The large water tower alongside supplied the water crane for the adjacent goods loop. The entrance to the ex-GWR locomotive depot and carriage sidings is on the left of the picture. 'Hall' No 5902 *Howick Hall* on an up freight supplies the motive power interest. *J. D. Edwards*

Bottom right:
The signalbox at Kennington Junction was unusual as it faced the branch and not the main line. 'Castle' class 4-6-0 No 7007 *Great Western* passes on a Hereford-Paddington train. *J. D. Edwards*

Right:
Oxford Road Junction seen from the A423 road bridge which was built during 1935. Prior to the provision of a bridge here, the road crossed the line on the flat by way of a level crossing, part of which can still be seen to the left of the picture. The signalbox was constructed during the late 1950s to replace an earlier box that had stood nearer to the milepost. The line to the left is for Oxford, to the right is the Yarnton loop. The date is 4 February 1958. *J. D. Edwards*

Above:
Accidents were few and far between in the Oxford area. However, on 25 September 1952 a goods train was derailed at Appleford Crossing, the worst casualty being Appleford Crossing signalbox, which, as can be seen, was completely demolished. *Ian Allan Library*

Left:
The interior of Oxford North Junction signalbox during the last night of operation, on 12 October 1973. Here Signalman Bill Culham operates a block instrument. Note the emergency oil lamps hanging from the roof. Oxford North Junction box was opened on 8 November 1940. *B. Higgins*

Bottom left:
Oxford panel box in October 1984, situated on the down platform. This small panel controls about 26 miles of track between Didcot North Junction and Heyford. It also controls some 13½ miles of track on the Cotswold line to Ascott-under-Wychwood. When it was commissioned on 13 October 1973 it replaced over a dozen manual signalboxes. *Author*

Development of Passenger Services

At the opening of the Oxford Railway, a service of 10 up trains per day was provided, with only the 7.50am train running through to London; all other trains terminated at Didcot, allowing the traveller to catch the up Exeter and Bristol expresses. Down trains ran in a similar fashion, with passengers again having to change at Didcot to catch the branch train, only the 7.30pm ran right through from London to Oxford. These two trains took 2hr 40min to complete the 62 miles, whereas changing at Didcot and catching a fast train allowed the traveller to complete the journey in 2hr 20min, which was certainly not fast by any standards. Criticisms of slow running throughout the GW system at this time had been mentioned in a Board of Trade Report of January 1845, during discussions regarding proposals for a broad gauge line from Oxford to Rugby and Wolverhampton. This criticism stung the GWR into taking immediate action, and on 10 February 1845 all the services were greatly speeded up; making it possible to travel from Oxford to London, including the change at Didcot, in only 1hr 15min, quite a remarkable change.

The old station at Oxford saw its last passengers in October 1852, and with the opening of the line to Birmingham a new service was inaugurated with two through trains each way timed to cover the 129 miles in only 2hr 45min; stopping only at Oxford and Leamington Spa. This gave a Paddington-Oxford time of 70min, with an average speed of 54mph, still via Didcot station, as the Didcot East avoiding line was not opened until 1856. These early trains were mainly in the hands of Gooch 'Iron Duke' class locomotives in their original form and for many years Oxford had an allocation of these fine locomotives for the fast services. These trains continued to run with only slight variation to the overall timing until October 1861 when the down broad gauge service to Birmingham was withdrawn and replaced with a new standard gauge service of three through trains each way; all were unfortunately slower than the earlier broad gauge timings. The down morning train took some 3hr 20min to reach Birmingham, which

was hardly an improvement. All ran non-stop from Paddington to Oxford via Didcot curve; Didcot station did not become mixed gauge until 1863. The up evening train, however, was one of the few broad gauge services still running from Birmingham, and that retained a timing of approximately 2hr 55min, about 25min faster than the new improved standard gauge service!

During 1869 the broad gauge rails north of Oxford were removed and all Birmingham trains reverted to standard gauge. These trains were for many years in the hands of Gooch-designed 2-2-2 locomotives Nos 69-76, built by Beyer Peacock in 1855, and also the Sharp engines Nos 157-166 built in 1862. It is interesting to note that some of the early Beyer Peacock locomotives, albeit in rebuilt form, were still working from Oxford during 1901.

One cannot discuss the early services without reference to the Shipton-on-Cherwell accident, one of the worst ever to have happened on the GWR. On Christmas Eve 1874, the 10am train from Paddington to Birmingham arrived at Oxford half an hour late due to fog in the Thames Valley. The train was hauled by Armstrong 2-2-2 No 478, together with 15 six-wheel coaches. The train was very crowded, with little third-class room, so a small four-wheel third-class coach, together with a second Armstrong engine No 386 of the same class was added at Oxford. This heavy train of two locomotives and 16 coaches left Oxford at 12.18pm. Soon after passing Woodstock Road station (now Kidlington) at about 35mph, the tyre of the small coach broke away and the coach became derailed. The drivers did not realise anything was wrong until the train was approaching Hampton Gay. They immediately shut off steam, reversed their engines and whistled for the guard to apply his brakes. The result was appalling: the small coach was crushed by the braking weight of the heavy train. Nine of the other coaches were derailed, falling down the steep bank; 34 people were killed and 65 injured. The small carriage, No 351, was an old West Midlands vehicle in poor condition; the tyres had apparently been repaired by fixing them

on with rivets through the rim of the wheel. Various rule changes were made as a result of the accident, outlawing this type of repair.

In 1880 the Birmingham service was accelerated once again with the 4.45pm down train timed at 2hr 45min, the same as the 1852 broad gauge schedule! During these later years the trains were in the hands of 'Queen' and 'Cobham' class locomotives. Between the years 1891-1902 continuous improvements were made to the timetable. Listed below is a brief summary of these:

July 1891. Additional services to Birmingham daily; three extra trains each way

July 1892. A new fast through train between Oxford and Southampton and vice versa via Didcot and Newbury

July 1896. 9.30am Paddington-Barmouth to run non-stop to Leamington Spa in 2hr and to reach Barmouth in 6hr 50min.
Also additional fast trains from Birmingham to Paddington.

July 1898. Above service quickened to run to Birmingham non-stop in 2hr 27min, reaching Barmouth in 6hr 27min.
New express to and from Cheltenham via Oxford and Chipping Norton Junction.

July 1900. 1.40pm Paddington-Worcester non-stop, reaching Worcester in 2hr 15min; a new train from Oxford to Westbury via Didcot West curve to meet the Weymouth boat train.

July 1902. A faster service to Birmingham non-stop taking just 2hr 20min with a new slip coach service to Leamington Spa in 1hr 35min by three trains per day.

Above:
'Cobham' or '157' class 2-2-2 No 158 designed by Gooch and built at Swindon in 1879. This locomotive, allocated to Oxford during 1904, was withdrawn in June 1905.
Real Photographs (15135)

Top right:
'City' class 4-4-0 No 3718 *City of Winchester* **gathers speed as she passes Hinksey Lake with a Worcester-Paddington train of the 1920s.**
L&GRP (12774)

Right:
No 7004 *Eastnor Castle* **at Kennington on an up Worcester-Paddington train. In the background stands the bridge that carries the Risborough branch over the Thames at this point.**
Dr G. Smith

Further changes to the service took place when the Birmingham cut-off line was opened in 1910 from Ashendon Junction to Aynho. From this date many of the Paddington-Birmingham trains disappeared from the Oxford line on to this new route, leaving only through cross-country trains and the Paddington-Oxford-Worcester service, with the odd Wolverhampton via Oxford working.

Although the London, Birmingham and Worcester services have always formed the backbone of the passenger traffic in Oxford, it is its association with the cross-country trains and the subsequent arrival of locomotives and stock from other regions that made it such an attractive rail centre for the enthusiast. When the general railway pattern had been laid down in the late 19th century, the various

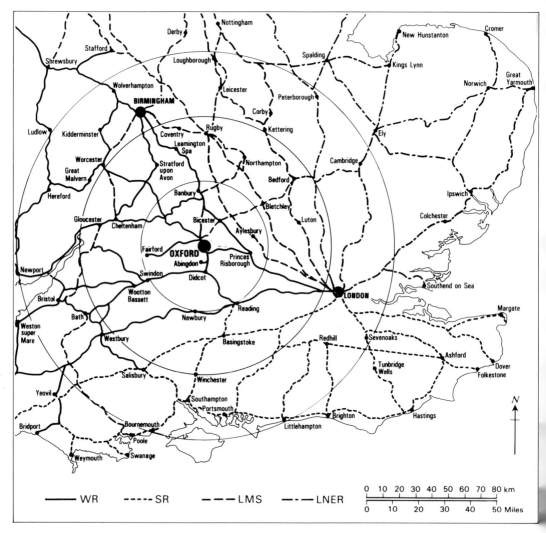

——— WR	----- SR	— — LMS	—·— LNER					

0 10 20 30 40 50 60 70 80 km

0   10   20   30   40   50 Miles

N

Above:
Rail routes from Oxford in pre-Nationalisation days.

companies started to include through coaches on many regular service trains; these coaches would be shunted on and off the services travelling across the country until the destination was reached, a time consuming and very slow process for the traveller. The mixing of the gauges south of Oxford had allowed through coaches from the north as early as 1856, but probably the most important development to the cross-country services was the opening of the joint GC/GW line to Banbury Junction in 1900. Within a short space of time through trains rather than the through carriages started to operate. Services such as Newcastle-Bournemouth and Leeds-Bristol were an early feature of the new connection. In

1902 improvements were made consisting of a new train from Swindon to Leicester which also included a through coach from Bristol, also a new buffet car express from York and Bradford to Oxford with through coaches to Bournemouth. This train was the forerunner of the York-Bournemouth that is still running today.

The GC timetable of 1903 showed four trains per day each way between Bournemouth and Sheffield via Oxford with subsequent connections further north and also a 7.45am Bristol-Nottingham service. By 1910 the service on to the GC through Oxford had increased to seven down and six up trains to Nottingham and beyond. These services were gradually improved and continued with little change until the beginning of World War 2 in 1939. An interesting feature of the 1920s and

Above:
**Unrebuilt 'West Country' Pacific No 34105
Swanage stands at Oxford station
platform with a train composed of ex-Southern
and LNER coaches and British Railways Mk 1
stock.** *J. A. Coiley*

Right:
**An unidentified 'Hall' passes through Oxford at
the head of a mixed rake of stock as No 6822
Manton Grange stands at the down platformn.**
R. C. Riley

930s had been the provision in 1921 of through carriages including sleepers between Penzance and Aberdeen, a distance of approximately 785 miles. The war years saw the withdrawal of many of the cross-country services, but during the postwar period many of the prewar timetables reappeared, although the Penzance-Aberdeen through carriages did not. This resurgence of cross-country services was short-lived, however, as the postwar austerity period up to 1947, together with the various fuel crises of 1950-51 onwards caused drastic cuts, many of the through trains disappearing for ever. The 1947 timetable shows only two weekday trains: the 7.10pm Swindon-Sheffield via Leicester GC, which left Oxford at 8.25pm, and the 8.10pm Sheffield-

Swindon, arriving at Oxford at 1.30am. Saturdays, however, still produced Bournemouth-Birmingham, Bournemouth-Birkenhead, Weymouth-Birmingham and Swindon-York trains.

One very interesting working was the Sundays only 9.20am Sheffield-Swansea via Woodford Halse and Banbury Junction. Starting from 7 January 1940, this train was

worked through to Swindon by LNER locomotives. The first to appear on the service was Class B17 4-6-0 No 2852 *Darlington*; more interesting were the various older Atlantics and GC locomotives, but these were well worn and unreliable. Eventually the newer 'B1' class took over. The train continued to run until the early 1960s, still handled by these ex-LNER 'B1' class locomotives, but the train now terminated at Swindon.

It was to be quite a few years before these cross-country services were again to run at the prewar frequency. The 1954 summer timetable illustrates this resurgence in traffic, the postwar depression had gone and we were all entering into an era of 'never having had it so good!'. The weekday timetable contained York-Swindon, Swansea-York, Bournemouth-Birkenhead, Birkenhead-Hastings and Dover, Weymouth-Wolverhampton and Bournemouth-York services, whilst the Saturday timetable easily doubled this list. Services of the late 1950s and early 1960s continued at this level. The 1964 weekday service consisted of a Bournemouth-Liverpool and Manchester train, a Bournemouth-York and an evening Swindon-Sheffield, each with a comparable return working. The 10am Bournemouth-Liverpool with a portion to Manchester

Piccadilly was certainly a forerunner of things to come, for dieselisation brought with it the advent of the InterCity image for British Rail. The early 1970s saw the gradual build-up of the cross-country services in the Oxford area and now into the mid 1980s there are more cross-country trains passing through Oxford than at any other time in its history.

Currently, these run from and to the following southern destinations: Brighton, Weymouth, Poole, Bournemouth and Portsmouth Harbour, and in a northerly direction from and to Derby, Liverpool, Manchester, Leeds, Newcastle, York, Bradford, Hull and Glasgow, the last being a particularly interesting train, leaving Poole at 07.34 and arriving at Glasgow Central at 16.37, a distance of some 489 miles. All of these trains now run Mondays-Saturdays, and continue to establish Oxford as a major cross-country rail centre.

Another very important aspect of local railway operations were the semi-fast stopping trains on the London, Birmingham and Worcester lines. These services provided connections to and from the express and cross-country trains at Oxford. The local outer London suburban service reached Oxford with an hourly service, stopping at most intermediate stations en route.

The Worcester line saw a reduced intermediate service as most of the Hereford-London trains also called at many of the stations north of Oxford, giving a two hourly service between 7.00am and 7.00pm. The smaller stations and halts between Banbury and Oxford were served by up to seven trains per day, three morning, three afternoon and

one in the late evening. The LNWR line to Bletchley was always operated on semi-fast nature with trains stopping at all stations en route.

These stopping services were operated from the opening of the respective lines, with many stations being provided over the ensuing years as possible patronage was anticipated. This was evident during 1905 with the introduction by the LNWR of a steam railmotor service to Bicester and in 1908 by the GWR to Heyford and also to Princes Risborough. To facilitate these services numerous small halts were opened by the respective companies. Unfortunately these services did not survive for long, the GWR service being withdrawn during 1915; the LNWR service lasted until 1926 although suffering a break during World War 1 from January 1917 until May 1919, being resumed during that month. A list of these halts can be found in the appendices. The introduction of GWR diesel railcars into the area during 1935 resurrected memories of these earlier railmotor services. Many of the long-closed railmotor halts were, however, never re-opened, only Horspath and Towersley on the Risborough line regaining a service.

Although working in the area until 1957, these diesel railcars were never really exploited to the full, something which the re-opening of the earlier halts might have achieved. The local services continued with both steam and diesel haulage until the rationalisation of the 1960s saw many of the small stations close. The whole of the ex-LNWR service to Bletchley closed during 1967. Many of the intermediate stations on the Banbury line were closed, with, at the time of writing, only Tackley, Heyford and King's Sutton remaining open. Luckily many of the stations on the Worcester line remain, with all stations south of Oxford to London surviving.

There is talk of a new station being provided at Kidlington, but to counteract this the future of King's Sutton appears to be in the balance. The future may also see trains once again on the Bletchley line but a considerable amount of local authority money will be needed for the provision of stations on this line.

The London Services

The fastest running to and from Oxford has always been to London, even the earliest broad gauge services show times of only 75min to and from the capital. Over the years these times have continued to be reduced and it is now possible to reach London by HST in only 44min. Some of these early services deserve mention for the fast running of certain trains.

The 1895 timetable shows the 9.30am, 11.25am and 2.15pm down trains from Paddington to Birkenhead timed to reach Oxford in only 68min, with the 1.40pm Worcester service with a slightly heavier load taking just 70min. These trains would usually be hauled by Gooch or Dean Single engines. On one such run, Dean 7ft 8in Single No 3058 *Grierson* with 10 coaches on the 1.40pm down Worcester lost two minutes due to a pw slack at Hayes, but still arrived at Oxford 1min earlier than its 70min schedule. This tradition of fast running on the London trains continued into the 20th century and a regular feature of the service during the 1920s and 1930s was the 10.10am up fast. This was worked by a Worcester crew with a 'Star' class engine, together with a regular load of 10 coaches. A scheduled time of 60min was allowed for this run, being beaten on many occasions. The return 12.45pm service to Worcester also had a 60min schedule to Oxford but it did not stop there on the down run. This service was discontinued during World War 2. After the war the fastest service from Oxford to London was the 2.15pm train from Wolverhampton forming the 5.35pm Oxford-Paddington. This also had a 60min schedule for its non-stop run to the capital. The demise of steam during the 1960s saw subsequent dieselisation of the services with a general reduction in journey times. The current timetable shows many fast runs; the 07.05 ex-Hereford, the 09.00 from Oxford is the fastest locomotive-hauled run, reaching London in just 53min. There are many sub-60min trains to London, even those including a stop at Reading. The Class 47 and 50 locomotives provided for these services regularly achieve early arrivals at the capital on one such occasion the author travelling on the 09.00 behind Class 50 No 50048 *Dauntless* arrived 7min early at Paddington. The fastest runs however are being achieved with the HSTs on the Oxford trains with two very fast services: the up 11.10 takes just 45min, with the fastest run scheduled on the down 13.35 a time of 44min being allowed for this run during 1985.

It is worth mentioning at this point that in 1985 London could be reached from Oxford by 33 services, with an equivalent number of down workings, but the traveller certainly had to pick the right service to use, for whereas in 13.35 HST took just 44min to reach London the 10.57 DMU took a staggering 2hr 22min to reach the same destination, albeit stopping at most stations en route!

What does the future hold for the Oxford London service? the possible electrification of

the Oxford line by the turn of the century will certainly speed up the semi-fast journey times, but it is hard to see some of the fine running times being achieved by the HSTs being beaten by much, if at all. It is remarkable to consider that in the time it took the 13.35 to reach Paddington in 1985, on the 5.35pm fast in 1960 you would still be travelling in the vicinity of Burnham and Slough!

Top:

'Castle' No 7007 *Great Western* leaves Oxford with the 12.15pm departure for Paddington on 2 July 1960. *K. L. Cook*

Above:

On 28 January 1975 Class 52 No 1023 *Western Fusilier* suffered a broken axle entering Oxford with the 14.05 Paddington-Birmingham, and left the rails with the first two coaches. *D. Parker*

Class 47 No 47372 accelerates away from Oxford with the 09.58 Manchester-Brighton, passing the site of Hinksey South yard on 20 July 1985. *Author*

Above:
HSTs now run into Oxford several times a day; they provide the fastest service to and from London. The 13.40 to Paddington leaves Oxford on its 45min trip. *Author*

Left:
Oxford North carriage sidings on a dull morning in 1984. Class 50 No 50005 *Collingwood* waits to form a commuter train to Paddington. Class 117 three-car suburban DMU L422 stands alongside. *T. E. J. Waters*

The Named Trains

The 'Cathedrals Express'

The resurgence of interest within the Western Region of the late 1950s produced an Indian summer of Western express running before the mass exodus to the scrap yard of many of the fine express locomotives and the subsequent dieselisation of the 1960s. Many of the crack named trains were formed of carriage stock repainted in the famous chocolate and cream, and the locomotives were turned out clean and green to complement the coaches. Some new named trains were introduced. The timetable of 1957 showed one of these for the Oxford line, the 'Cathedrals Express'. This title was given to the 7.45am up Hereford, Oxford and Paddington, and the 4.45pm down.

The locomotive carried a headboard suitably inscribed 'Cathedrals Express', over which was a bishop's mitre. The 1957 loading for the train was 10 coaches, but by 1959 this had been reduced to eight British Railways Mk 1s, suitably painted in chocolate and cream. The up 'Cathedrals' covered the Worcester-London section in only 2¼hr, the Oxford-Paddington section, non-stop, was accomplished in 68min. The down train, however, included stops at Moreton-in-Marsh, and Evesham, taking a slightly longer time of 2hr 21min.

In the early 1960s the train was re-timed, with an 8.00am departure from Hereford, with arrival at Oxford at 10.37am. The service now included a stop at Reading with the up journey time subsequently increased to 76min. The down train, however, did not include the Reading stop; it left Paddington at 5.15pm and 72min were allowed for the non-stop run to Oxford. The 'Cathedrals' was, however, to be short-lived, and the name was dropped from the 1964 timetable with the takeover of the Worcester trains by diesel traction.

The table below shows a run on the up 'Cathedrals' on Tuesday 22 October 1957. The train was 1½min late departing from Oxford, a fine run was made, resulting in 1¼min early arrival at Paddington.

Oxford-Paddington. Tuesday 22 October 1957. 'Cathedrals Express'

Locomotive: 'Castle' class No 7005 *Sir Edward Elgar*
Load: 10 coaches; 340 ton tare, 360 ton gross
Schedule: 68min

Distance m-ch	Location	Actual min sec	Speed mph
0.00	OXFORD	0.0	0.0
2.05	Kennington Junction	4.30	
5.00	Radley	7.30	60
7.25	Culham	10.00	60
8.03	Appleford	11.00	60
10.00	Didcot	13.00	60
14.09	Cholsey	18.30	53*
18.65	Goring	22.00	64
21.09	Pangbourne	25.10	62
24.75	Tilehurst	27.50	62
27.40	Reading	30.30	62
32.04	Twyford	35.00	67
39.15	Maidenhead	40.45	70
40.09	Taplow	42.15	70
42.04	Burnham	43.35	68
44.09	Slough	45.40	72
47.15	Langley	47.33	72
48.65	Iver	48.52	56†
50.02	West Drayton	50.16	61
52.05	Hayes	52.21	65
54.04	Southall	54.18	62
56.05	Hanwell	56.02	61
57.65	Ealing Broadway	57.36	59
60.65	Old Oak Common	61.16	—
62.15	Westbourne Park	62.50	—
63.35	PADDINGTON	66.11	—

*=Speed Restriction   †=Signal

Left:
The 1960 timetable for the 'Cathedrals Express'.
Author's collection

Table 14

THE
CATHEDRALS
EXPRESS

RESTAURANT CAR SERVICE

LONDON, OXFORD,
WORCESTER and HEREFORD

WEEK DAYS

		pm				am
London (Paddington)	.. .. dep	4A45	Hereford .. .. dep	7A45
Oxford .. .. { arr	5 58	Ledbury .. .. ,,	8 6
	dep	6 4	Colwall .. .. ,,	8 16
Moreton-in-Marsh .. .. .. arr	6 41	Malvern Wells.. .. .. .. ,,	8 21
Evesham .. .. ,,	7 0	Great Malvern .. .. ,,	8A25
Worcester (Shrub Hill).. .. ,,	7 20	Malvern Link .. .. ,,	8 29
Fernhill Heath .. .. .. arr	dd	Worcester (Foregate Street){ arr	8 40
Droitwich Spa .. .. .. ,,	7 46	{ dep	8 42
Hartlebury .. .. ,,	7 56	Worcester (Shrub Hill).. .. arr	8 45
Kidderminster .. .. .. ,,	8 3	Kidderminster .. .. .. dep	8A20
		Droitwich Spa .. .. .. ,,	8A32
Worcester (Shrub Hill).. .. dep	7 29		
Worcester (Foregate Street).. ,,	7 32	Worcester (Shrub Hill) .. .. dep	8A55
Malvern Link .. .. .. arr	7 43	Evesham .. .. ,,	9 12
Great Malvern.. .. .. .. ,,	7 47	Moreton-in-Marsh .. .. .. ,,	9 36
Colwall .. .. ,,	7 56	Oxford .. .. { arr	10 10
Ledbury .. .. ,,	8 7	{ dep	10 15
Hereford .. .. ,,	8 30	London (Paddington) .. .. arr	11 25

A—Seats can be reserved in advance on payment of a fee of 2s. 0d. per seat (see page 23).

dd—Calls to set down passengers on notice to the Guard.

Above:

Yarnton Junction station, with 'Castle' class No 4088 *Dartmouth Castle* on the down 'Cathedrals Express'. The track in the foreground is the entrance to the Witney branch. Part of the yard provided here during World War 2 can be seen in the right-hand background.
J. D. Edwards

Below:

The down 'Cathedrals Express' at Oxford in 1957 hauled by 'Castle' No 7026 *Tenby Castle*.
B. Higgins

The 'Pines Express'

There was only one other named train which regularly ran on the Oxford line: the 'Pines Express'. This had been running between Manchester and Bournemouth for many years, using the Somerset & Dorset route through from Bath. From 9 September 1962, however, the train was re-routed via Oxford and Reading West and continued to run on this route until 1967 when, like many other named trains throughout the country it was withdrawn from the timetable. During its days of running on the Oxford line both up and down trains changed engines at Oxford. Motive power to and from the South was usually in the form of either a Bulleid 'Merchant Navy' or 'West Country' class locomotive. However, from January 1966 the engine change took place at Banbury as by this time Oxford depot had closed. This through running to Banbury continued until the 1966 summer timetable ended, thereafter the service was operated by diesel traction.

The 'Oxford Pullman'

The timetable for 1967 showed a new afternoon Pullman service from London to Oxford. Using one of the Western Region's Pullman diesel sets, this train was christened the 'Oxford Pullman', although it never actually carried the name. Leaving the capital at 12.15pm and taking just 60min to reach Oxford, returning again at 4.15pm, the idea was to attract visitors to Oxford, Americans in particular. Unfortunately the tourist patronage did not materialise and the train was discontinued during 1969.

Below:
This interesting picture shows one of the new Western Region Diesel Pullman trains on a test run to Oxford during May 1960, prior to entering service on the Birmingham and Bristol routes. These trains did not appear in revenue service on the Oxford line until 1967 when the short-lived 'Oxford Pullman' workings commenced.
J. D. Edwards

The 'Cotswold Line'

The rundown of the Oxford Worcester & Wolverhampton Railway Line from Oxford, known today as the 'Cotswold Line', probably started with the closure of the Yarnton loop during 1965. This had provided an important freight connection for the proposed East Anglia-South Wales route, which necessitated the building of the flyover at Bletchley during the early 1960s. The subsequent abandonment by British Rail of this link together with the removal of the loop meant an end to this traffic. Between 1965 and 1966 passenger services took a knock when a number of the smaller stations on the line were closed. 1969 also saw Honeybourne succumb, and the future of the whole line was obviously in the balance.

The line briefly came to the public eye, when on Saturday 30 January 1965 Sir Winston Churchill was buried at Bladon. His body was carried by a special train for the 78-mile journey from Waterloo to Handborough. This station was only a short distance from Bladon Church, his own choice of resting place. The train was worked throughout the journey by Bulleid Pacific No 34051 *Winston Churchill*, which ran into the up platform by way of a temporary crossover.

With rationalisation in the early 1970s, over 40 of the 57 miles between Oxford and Worcester were singled and once again there was much speculation about imminent closure, made firmer in 1978 by the decision to remove all but two of the locomotive-hauled through trains. This was due to the deteriorating state of the track. Lightweight DMUs formed the bulk of the services, and passengers were required to change at Oxford to gain main line connections. It was around this time that the commuters, together with local inhabitants along the line, formed the Cotswold Line Promotion Group to 'publicise, safeguard and improve rail and bus feeder

services along the Oxford-Worcester line'; on all these scores they have been extremely successful. During 1981 Honeybourne station was reopened, and gradually the trackwork throughout the route has been brought up to 95mph main line standards again. The timetable for 1985 shows two early morning up locomotive-hauled trains to London, these being the 06.00 and 07.00 ex-Hereford, with two evening returns the 17.05 and 18.07 to Hereford. An additional train, the 19.03 ex-Paddington, runs on Fridays but only as far as Worcester Shrub Hill. An interesting development for the 1984/85 timetable was the introduction of an HST set as far as Great Malvern, aptly named the 'Cotswold and Malvern Express'. It leaves the capital at 10.10 and takes just 2hr 5min, reaching Worcester at 12.02 and arriving in Great Malvern at 12.15.

The up journey leaves Great Malvern at 13.12, and reaches Paddington at 15.24. For the 1985 summer timetable, the early morning 07.00 has been named the 'Cathedrals Express' — memories of 1957 once again.

Certainly with these improvements the future of the Cotswold Line now looks quite secure, and with a steady increase in usage travellers should continue to enjoy a trip along this most scenic of routes for many years to come.

A less encouraging development in late 1985 was the announcement of the abolition of the Oxford Area in Western Region management from 1986. This meant that the 'Cotswold Line' which had previously been under the wing of the Oxford Area Manager would henceforth be divided between the Reading and Gloucester Areas; a far from satisfactory state of affairs.

Above:
Class 35 'Hymek' diesel-hydraulic No 7030 passes Wolvercote Junction with the 13.15 Paddington-Hereford on 2 October 1971. For several years these Type 3 locomotives were regular motive power on this line. *T. G. Flinders*

Right:
For the summer 1985 timetable the 07.00 Hereford-Paddington has regained the title 'Cathedrals Express'. Here on 13 May 1985, the newly-named No 47627 *City of Oxford* carries the 'Cathedrals Express' headboard. The train had earlier been blessed en route by the Bishops of Hereford and Oxford. *Author*

The Railcar Era

Above right:

Abingdon Road halt, one of six new halts built by the Great Western Railway in 1908 for the steam railmotor service to Princes Risborough, all of which closed when the railmotor service ceased in 1915. This picture is taken from the Red Bridge on the old Abingdon Road, south of Oxford. The chimney on the distant left is of Sandford Mill, now demolished. The green fields on the right are now engulfed by the urban housing of Kennington, and the whole scene has now been bisected by the Oxford ring road. *L&GRP (8491)*

Below right:

Wolvercot platform, taken around 1911 when the GWR steam railmotors were working in the area. This small halt together with several others to the south of Oxford was opened in 1908. It is interesting to note that the GWR always spelt Wolvercot without a final 'e', whereas the usual spelling today is 'Wolvercote'. The LNWR, who also had a halt here, spelt it 'Woolvercot'.
F. Snow

Below:

In October 1905 the LNWR inaugurated a steam railmotor service from Oxford Rewley Road to Bicester. A number of small halts were opened to supplement this service. The picture above shows one of these prior to public opening with a railmotor on a test run. The halt is almost certainly at Wendlebury near Bicester.
Lens of Sutton

Opposite page:

Timetables and fares for some of the Great Western Railway railmotor services.
Author's collection

FARES. (3rd Class.)

FROM	Oxford.	Hinksey Halt.	Abingdon Road Halt.	Iffley Halt.	Littlemore.	Garsington Bridge Halt.	Horsepath Halt.	Wheatley.	Tiddington.	Thame.	Bledlow.
	s. d.	s. d.	s. d.	s. d.	s. d.	s. d.	s. d.	s. d.	d.	d.	d.
Hinksey Halt	1½	—									
Abingdon Road Halt	2	1	—								
Iffley Halt	2½	1½	1½	—							
Littlemore	3	2	1½	1	—						
Garsington Bridge Halt	5	3½	3	2½	1½	—					
Horsepath Halt	6	5	4½	3	3	1½	—				
Wheatley	8	6½	6	5	4½	3	1½	—			
Tiddington	11	10	9½	8	8	6½	5	3½	—		
Thame	1 3½	1 2	1 1½	1 0	1 0	10½	9	7½	4	—	
Bledlow	1 7½	1 6	1 5½	1 5	1 4	1 2½	1 1	11½	8	4	—
Princes Risborough	1 9	1 8	1 7	1 6½	1 6	1 5½	1 4	1 3	1 1	10	1½

FROM	Oxford.	Wolvercot Halt.	Kidlington.	Blenheim & Woodstock.	Bletchington.	FROM	Oxford.	Yarnton.	Handborough.	Charlbury.	Ascott-under-Wychwood.
	s. d.	d.	d.	d.	d.		s. d.	s. d.	d.	d.	d.
Wolvercot Halt	2	—				Yarnton	4	—			
Kidlington	5½	3½	—			Handborough	7	3	—		
Blenheim & Woodstock	9	7	3½	—		Charlbury	1 1	9½	6	—	
Bletchington	7½	5½	2	6	—	Ascott-under-Wychwood	1 5	1 1	10	3½	—
Heyford	1 0	9½	6	10	4	Shipton	1 6	1 2½	11	5	1½

OXFORD AND HEYFORD.

WEEK DAYS.

		M K		M T	T	M		M	M			M	M		
	a.m.	a.m.		a.m.	a.m.	a.m.	p.m.	p.m.		p.m.	p.m.	p.m.	p.m.	p.m.	
OXFORD dep.	7 50	8 12	...	9 4	10 35	11 35	12 17	1 57	...	3 25	...	...	6 30	9 20	
Wolvercot Halt ,,		8 18	...	9 30			12 23	2 3			4 10	5 41	...		
Kidlington ,,	8 5	8 27	...	9 39	10 47	11 45	12 31	2 11	...	3 35	4 19	5 49	6 42	9 30	
Blenheim & Woodstock arr.	8 40	8 40			11 2	12 2	1 23	2 19		3 54		6 27	7 0	9 43	
Bletchington dep.	8 11	8 32			10 53	11 50	12 38			3 42			6 48	9 36	
Heyford arr.	8 20	8 44			11 0	11 59	12 48			3 51			6 59	9 45	

		T	M K	M T		M	M		M	M		M	M	
	a.m.		a.m.	a.m.	a.m.	p.m.	p.m.		p.m.	p.m.		p.m.	p.m.	
Heyford dep	7 55	...	9 21	9 3	...	11 24	12 53	...	...	3 26	...	...	6 35	8 36
Bletchington ,,	8 6	...	9 29	9 31		11 32	1 4			3 34	...		6 44	8 45
Blenheim & Woodstock ,,	7 53	...	9 25	9 2	9 25	11 24	12 57	2 50		3 18	...	5 37	6 20	8 30
Kidlington ,,	8 15	...	9 36	9 3	9 41	11 39	1 10	3 0		3 42	4 23	5 55	6 50	8 50
Wolvercot Halt ,,		...		9 45	9 49		1 19	3 8		...	4 32	6 4	...	
OXFORD arr.	8 28	...	9 46	9 53	9 55	11 48	1 28	3 15		3 54	4 38	6 10	7 0	9 0

K Thursdays excepted. **M** Rail Motor Car, one class only. **T** Thursdays only.

OXFORD AND SHIPTON.

WEEK DAYS.

	a.m.	n'n.	p.m.	p.m.	p.m.	p.m.	p.m.		a.m.	a.m.	p.m.	p.m.	p.m.	p.m.
OXFORD dep.	8 5	12 0	2 25	3 44	6 15	7 36	8 55	Shipton (for Burford) dep	7 57	..	12 1	12 56	4 47	8 30
Yarnton ,,	8 14	X		3 53	R	R	R	Ascott-under-Wychwood ,,	8 2	..	12 5		4 51	8 34
Handboro' ,,	8 22	12 15	2 37	4 1	6 26	7 50	8 13	Charlbury ,,	8 10	10 32	12 15	1 5	4 59	8 43
Charlbury ,,	8 34	12 25	2 48	4 13	6 37	8 1	9 25	Handboro' ,,	8 21	10 43	12 27	1 16	5 13	8 56
Ascott-under-Wychwood ,,	8 41	12 35	....	4 20	....	8 8	9	Yarnton ,,	R	R	12 35		5 20	R
Shipton (for Burford) arr.	8 46	12 40	2 57	4 25	6 45	8 13	9 36	OXFORD arr	8 33	10 55	12 45	1 30	5 33	9 10

O Calls to set down Passengers from London and Oxford on notice being given by the Passenger to the Guard at Oxford. **R** Passengers from or to Yarnton travel via Oxford.
X Calls to set down Passengers on notice to Guard at Oxford, or to pick up Passengers upon notice being given at the Station before 11.45 a.m.

Development of Goods Services

From the arrival of the railway in Oxford, goods traffic has always formed an important part of the local railway operations. On the opening of the Oxford branch much of this was carried on mixed trains, with large amounts of coal and livestock being moved. The opening of the line to Wolverhampton in 1852 saw the industrial Midlands opened up to the GWR with a subsequent increase in traffic. It was the mixing of the gauges south of Oxford, during 1856 that had the greatest repercussions for goods traffic at this time, as trains could now travel for long distances without the problems of a gauge interchange. One such service inaugurated soon after this date was the Basingstoke-Victoria Basin, a service that was still operating over 100 years later.

Continued growth during the latter half of the 19th century saw the number of goods trains passing daily through Oxford increase progressively from 49 in 1858, 78 in 1876 to 98 in 1898. Some of these such as the 5.30pm Exeter-Birmingham and the 2.00am Basingstoke-Manchester were quite long distance hauls.

The opening of the GC connection to Banbury at the turn of the century, saw a considerable increase in the amount of coal traffic both passing through and using the small yards at Oxford, which at this time were situated at Oxford North, Becket Street and Rewley Road on the LNWR side. Rather surprisingly World War 1 did not cause the amount of goods traffic to rise dramatically in the area; it was to take another conflict in 1939 to do that.

World War 2 probably had a greater effect on the railway locally than any other period. In 1940 a new junction was opened between the GWR and the LNWR lines at Oxford North, and together with the building of a new ordnance depot at Bicester greatly increased through traffic on this line. The completion during 1942 of a new 1,000 wagon capacity yard at Hinksey now allowed a greater amount of goods traffic to be sorted locally. During these early years of the war, lines in the area often reached saturation point and to try to alleviate this problem new relief sidings were installed at many places locally. The major build up of supplies for the D-Day landings in Europe, saw Oxford reach an all-time record for the movement of goods, when during one week in April 1944 over 1,200 goods and military trains passed through the area.

The end of hostilities saw the traffic revert back to the prewar level of approximately 150 goods trains per day, with about 120 of these using the local yards. This total continued well into the 1950s. Once again there were some interesting runs at this time, examples being the 5.40am Sheffield-Bristol, the 9.25am Exeter-Oxley and the 12.05am Tavistock Junction-Woodford Halse; all calling at Hinksey, which at this time was still being shunted 24hr per day.

The growth of oil traffic in the late 1950s also produced many workings to and from Fawley Refinery near Southampton, with trains using both the Worcester and Birmingham routes from Oxford.

The removal of much goods traffic on to the roads has seen many of the local yards close for good. Yarnton and Rewley Road are now but a memory. Becket Street South still survives, but only just, whilst Hinksey is now reduced to a few exchange sidings at the North End. Cowley, however, continues to flourish and is described in the Wycombe Railway section. A list of current goods workings in the area can be found in the appendices.

Top right:
Viewed at the turn of the century, the small yard at Oxford Station South shows the cattle and horse dock. The whole site looks considerably tidier than it does now, being something of an eyesore currently with a motor vehicle scrap yard currently occupying the same area.
Minn collection Bodleian Library

Right:
The evening sun catches 'Modified Hall' No 6967 *Willesley Hall* near Appleford with a southbound freight on 28 August 1964. *Gerald T. Robinson*

Top:
Oxford North Junction during World War 2 with USA class S160 2-8-0 No 1871 leaving GW metals via the junction to take the ex-LNWR line to Bletchley. Oxford North goods yard, removed during the 1945 shed yard remodelling, can be seen to good effect at the right of the picture.
R. H. G. Simpson

Above:
Class 2884 No 3808 with a down freight near Kennington Junction. *R. C. Riley*

Top:
The 3.35pm Swindon-Hull and Grimsby fish empties always provided an ex-works engine on a running-in turn, and apart from 'Kings', almost every type of Western tender engine could be seen on this working. When it arrived at Oxford around 4.45pm, many spotters ensured that this was the one train of the day not to be missed. It was of course easy to tell if you had, from the obnoxious smell that lingered after its passing. In 1961 a beautifully clean 'Castle' No 4074 *Caldicot Castle* runs into Oxford past Hinksey yard. *A. Simpkins*

Above:
'Modified Hall' class No 6971 *Athelhampton Hall* on a Wolverhampton train waits to enter Oxford station, at a spot unofficially named 'Graveyard Halt' by generations of commuters who had to, and still do sit alongside the cemetery to wait for a clear road into the down platform. The Great Western goods shed in the background was built during the 1860s and removed in 1984. Note the crates of Morris car parts in the four-wheel wagons standing on the up loop. *J. D. Edwards*

Left:

Former War Department 2-8-0 No 90516 of Woodford Halse shed moves a Woodford-Hinksey freight past the south end of the up platform and over the Botley Road bridge. The up platform inspection pit can be seen just to the right of the first few trucks, between the track. Surprisingly the down platform did not have this facility. *J. D. Edwards*

Centre left:

From their introduction in 1954, the Standard '9F' 2-10-0 locomotives were always regular visitors to Oxford, with Midland Division locomotives coming from Toton, Wellingborough and Saltley; Western Region examples from Old Oak Common and Banbury. In 1963 several examples were allocated to Oxford, including for a short time No 92220 *Evening Star*, the last steam locomotive to be built at Swindon Works. No 92137 of Saltley (Birmingham) takes the up through road at Oxford with an empty oil train from the Midlands to Fawley refinery on an August day in 1962. *W. Turner*

Below:

Near the end of steam operation, a very neglected 'Modified Hall' No 6964 *Thornbridge Hall* makes heavy weather of hauling its up freight past Kennington Junction signalbox on 17 August 1965. The locomotive is devoid of all name and numberplates. *Ian Allan Library*

Above:
North British Locomotive Co Type 2 diesel-hydraulic No D6350 moves through Oxford with a Hinksey-Banbury North yard freight. The diamond crossing on the down side is clearly visible, although by 1967 (the year of this picture) little used. NBL Type 2 diesels, which became Class 22, regularly worked in the Oxford area until their subsequent withdrawal by the beginning of 1972. D6350 was an early casualty, being withdrawn in September 1968.
Author's collection

Centre right:
English Electric Type 4 No D217 *Carinthia* pulls into the loop at Oxford South yard with the 16.55 Banbury-Oxford freight on 5 April 1968.
D. A. Idle

Bottom right:
Southern Region BRC&W Type 3 No D6583 hauls a train of shining new oil tankers past the dilapidated Oxford station on 14 September 1963. *R. A. Panting*

Above:
Oxford is quite often used as a diversionary
route when other lines are closed; one such
occasion was on Sunday 16 September 1979
when closure of the Lickey incline saw a number
of Radyr-Corby coal trains diverted via Oxford.
Here Class 25 locomotives Nos 25134 and 25212
move one such train northward through
Oxford. *B. Daniels*

Left:
Looking south from the Red Bridge at Hinksey, a
Class 56 waits in the down loop. Compare this
picture with the earlier view of Abingdon Road
halt; both are taken from the same spot, 70 years
apart! *Author*

Top right:
On 22 March 1976, Class 46 No 46054 passes
through Oxford southwards to Hinksey yard
with a freight from the Bicester line. This
telephoto shot shows to great effect the tower of
St Barnabas church, Jericho, built in 1871; a
notable landmark for railway photographers at
Oxford. *P. E. Bailey*

The Oxford Gas, Light and Coke Co

No book regarding the railway in Oxford would be complete without including the above company, because for many years it operated its own internal standard gauge railway system connecting the old North gasworks to the new South gasworks and, via an exchange siding, to the Great Western main line. These sidings were situated approximately ½ mile south of Oxford station.

The Oxford Gas, Light and Coke Co was founded in 1818 when a small gasworks was established on land north of the River Thames in an area known locally as St Ebbes. In 1819 Oxford city received its first gas street lighting. Continued expansion over the years saw the number of consumers rise to 3,690 in 1882. By this time the North works had been extended from the original two acres to five acres and continued expansion on this site was impossible. The company sought and gained approval under the Oxford Gas Act of 1882 to extend their site to land south of the river. Approval was also given at that time to construct a railway system and a new river bridge to connect the old works to the new site and also to the GWR main line south of the river. This connection was completed in 1886.

In 1919 the new plant was finally installed on the south site and gas started to be produced in 1926. By this time the number of consumers had risen to 12,695, and the gas making capacity of the complete works had risen to three million cubic feet per day. In 1930 the company expanded further by taking over the Abingdon gasworks, and in the same year changed its name to the Oxford and District Gas Co. Under the Nationalisation Act of 1948 the company lost its individual status and became part of the Southern Gas Board. The gasworks were closed by the SGB in 1960 and demolished soon after. At the height of its production the gasworks covered a total area of some 19 acres.

The railway that the company had installed connecting the two plants consisted of private sidings some two miles in total within the works boundaries. These sidings over the years were worked by small 0-4-0 saddle tanks of both Peckett and Bagnall design. They were the property of the gas company, but interestingly from November 1924 to February 1925 the company hired from the Great Western Railway an ex-Taff Vale 0-4-0ST, No 1342 with a view to purchasing the same.

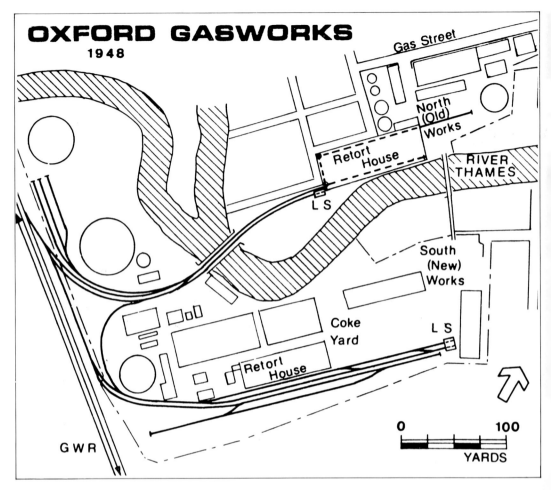

OXFORD GASWORKS
1948

Gas Street

North
(Old)
Works

Retort House

RIVER
THAMES

L S

South
(New)
Works

Coke
Yard

L S

Retort
House

GWR

0   100

YARDS

This locomotive was available for sale by the Great Western Railway; by this time, however, it was getting rather old, having been manufactured in 1876 by Hudswell Clarke. The gas company eventually decided against buying this 49-year old engine and instead purchased a brand new Peckett No 1682. The four locomotives owned by the company during this century were as follows:

0-4-0ST W. Bagnall 1839 Built 1906 (wdn 1949)
0-4-0ST Peckett   1682 Built 1925 (wdn 1960)
0-4-0ST W. Bagnall 2656 Built 1942 (wdn 1957)
0-4-0ST Peckett   2075 Built 1946 (wdn 1960)

Generally speaking the Bagnalls operated in the old works, and the Pecketts in the new works.

During the winter months the exchange sidings received one train-load of coal per day, from either South Yorkshire or Derbyshire. These wagons would then be moved throughout this large system by these diminu-tive saddle tank engines. Today this site is empty and unused, although the connecting bridge across the Thames has survived and has been restored by the council to its original condition. Gas for Oxford is now supplied by pipeline from Southampton feeding a large storage tank situated at Cowley.

Above:
Map of the gas works railway in 1948.
Courtesy Industrial Railway Society

Above right:
Oxford Gas Co 0-4-0ST No 1839 built by William Bagnall Ltd and purchased by the gas company when new in 1906. She survived on the gas works railway until withdrawn in 1949. *J. B. Stoyel*

Right:
Always known as the 'New Engine', Oxford & District Gas Co Peckett 0-4-0ST No 2075, built in 1946. This engine saw service on the gas railway until its withdrawal in 1960 when the works themselves also closed. *J. B. Latham*

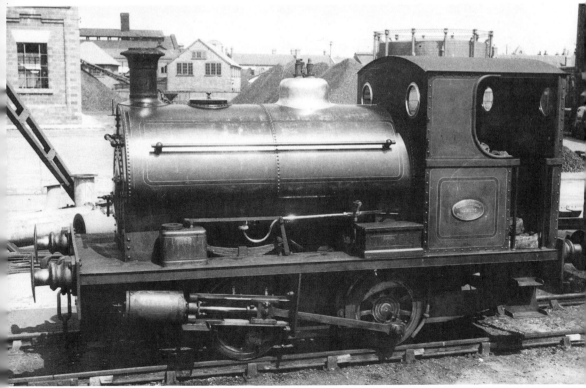

Oxford Today

Oxford has suffered, as have many other parts of the system, with the removal of much of the evidence of an earlier railway age. Passengers arriving at Oxford station today may well seek for some visible signs of this earlier, historic side of the railway. Alas, they would have to look long and hard to find anything locally. The modern railway with its InterCity image does not dwell on the past; and Oxford has proved to be no exception in having much of its early railway inheritance removed. On the GWR side almost everything has gone, but fortunately the LNWR is still represented with the historic swing bridge and the remains of the Rewley Road terminus. The last major GWR building in the area, the goods shed to the south of the station, was removed at the end of 1984. The GWR monogrammed wrought iron gates at the entrance to the South yard where this large shed once stood are still *in situ*, but apart from these it seems almost impossible to believe that Oxford, with its long GW traditions, now has little visible evidence left of this great company.

The station provided at Oxford today comprises two through platforms, with one down bay which is situated on the north up side. The old down bay had been removed in the early 1970s to provide a new road access to the nearby diesel depot, now closed. The downside platform nowadays contains a small buffet and waiting room together with some office accommodation and the Oxford MAS

powerbox. Many of the passenger facilities and administrative offices are situated on the up platform. Here a large refreshment room stands alongside the main station entrance, together with the ticket office and travel centre. The Area Manager's Office was also housed on this platform. From March 1986 certain down services calling at Oxford used the up platform, to avoid passengers having to use the congested and inconvenient subway.

What was in any case only ever intended as a temporary structure, with a planned life-span of approximately 10 years, has since proved to be inadequate for today's travellers. The area adjacent to the entrance lobby and ticket barrier becomes increasingly congested at various times throughout the day.

The combined effect of two trains arriving at both up and down platforms at the same time can result in total chaos for the travelling public at the one ticket collection barrier. The delay at this point often causes long queues to form along the subway, and in the entrance hall, resulting in frustration for passengers trying to enter and leave the platforms. This problem is clearly illustrated on Friday

Left:
The GWR monogram on the gates to Becket Street yard to the south of Oxford. One of the few remaining relics of that company still left at Oxford. *Author*

Top right:
On 22 January 1985 the Post Office released a set of five railway stamps entitled 'Famous Trains' based on paintings by Terence Cuneo. To publicise the occasion the carriage stock of the 'Venice Simplon Orient Express' hauled by Class 47 No 47500 *Great Western* travelled from Marylebone to Didcot Railway Centre via Wycombe, Banbury (reverse) and Oxford. Here the special stamp train leaves Oxford for Didcot. *Author*

Right:
The north end of Oxford up platform in 1985. When the station was rebuilt in 1970, all of the original platform covering was removed except for this portion of which the original support was retained and reroofed. *Author*

evenings when between 17.10 and 17.43 no fewer than eight very heavily loaded services arrive and depart. The sheer mass of people moving through the station at this time has to be seen to be appreciated. Some of the delays at the ticket barrier have now been alleviated by the introduction of an open station policy at Oxford. The small travel centre situated on the up side has also seen a growth in usage which was certainly not envisaged when it was

opened in 1975. A staff of just five deal with a conservative estimate of approximately 400,000 enquiries each year. Certainly with passengers nowadays able to book right through to the continent, the need for larger accommodation and improved facilities for this busy office is rapidly becoming a necessity.

This, together with the general poor design of the entrance and exit to the platforms has resulted in much talk regarding the rebuilding of the whole structure. In fact, it is interesting to see how history tends to repeat itself, for just as the 1852 station was rebuilt in 1890 because it proved inadequate for the passengers' needs, so the 1971 station seems to be heading for the same fate, and who knows, we may well see a new station by 1990!

It has already been mentioned that 1985 saw the removal of the GWR goods shed at Oxford South yard to provide a site for a small industrial development. This re-use of redundant railway land is also likely to see the Rewley Road site go over to industrial and commercial use in the near future. Now that the main freight terminal has been established at Cowley, this type of development could also bring about the closure of the remaining two small South yards.

The responsibility for the running of the railway locally was until 1986 in the hands of the Area Manager David Mather. His territory currently extended from Oxford to Worcester including much of the line to Hereford. He had a complete say over timetabling, staffing levels and local expenditure over this large area, some 130 route miles. The general upturn in business at both Oxford and Worcester is now producing an annual revenue for both passenger and freight traffic of about £15 million.

Oxford continues to be a busy centre for cross-country workings, producing many interesting through passenger trains. One of these — the 07.34 Poole-Glasgow — also contains a portion for Edinburgh and Dundee. For the 1985 summer timetable its was named the 'Wessex Scot'.

Interesting summer workings include the 08.05 Newcastle-Portsmouth Harbour 'SAGA Holiday train'; the down service leaving Portsmouth at 11.05. Many relief trains are also regular features during the summer months, with frequent Wolverhampton/ Birmingham-Poole and Weymouth workings supplementing the regular services.

Unfortunately with effect from the summer 1986 timetable the Manchester-Brighton trains were diverted away from the Oxford line to the West Coast route. Here they now travel as far as Willesden, where they gain access to the Southern via Kensington Olympia. Hopefully the gap in the timetable at Oxford will be filled with a new North-South service.

Problems on the West Coast main line in the London area on two recent occasions have seen the Oxford line used as a diversionary route. The blockage at Wembley on 12 October 1984 brought many extra trains on to the Oxford line, of which probably the most interesting was the up 'Clansman' which appeared with No 47598 hauling dead electric No 87028 *Lord President*. A second blockage at Watford on 11 May 1985 again saw many diversions passing through Oxford, and although no electric locomotives appeared this time the 01.15 Holyhead-Euston passed through hauled by freight engine No 58016, later returning north on the 10.20 Euston-Stranraer. On the same day an hourly service was provided from Paddington to Oxford and Wolverhampton.

Apart from these emergency services, there are other regular Sunday diversions through Oxford during the winter months. In 1985 these produced one locomotive-hauled service, the 23.50 Glasgow-Bristol sleeper, usually powered by a Class 45. The five other regular diversions are all HSTs; these are the 08.50

Leeds-Paignton, the 07.25 and 09.20 Bristol-Newcastle and the 09.45 and 10.30 Bristol-Manchester services. All of these use this route from the beginning of January until the start of the summer service, gaining access to and from the Bristol main line via Foxhall Junction, Didcot.

Apart from these extra workings, as described in the Motive Power chapter, most passenger turns these days are in the hands of just two types of locomotive. The electric train heating-equipped Class 47/4 locomotives provide the power for most of the cross-country workings, with Crewe, Bescot and Cardiff depots providing the bulk of the locomotives. However, examples from Eastfield, Gateshead and Immingham are also regular visitors. The Paddington-Oxford commuter trains, together with the Hereford services are still worked almost exclusively by Class 50s. The recently introduced 17.27 Paddington-Banbury is also rostered for Class 50 haulage, as is the Saturdays only 07.00 Oxford-Paignton. The HSTs continue to make off-peak appearances on both the Oxford-Paddington and Malvern-Paddington services, providing the fastest runs to and from the capital. The humble DMU does not draw much attention these days, but an interesting working brings a Cardiff-based set into Oxford each day. It arrives on what is effectively a Cardiff-Reading via Hereford and Oxford through service, leaving Cardiff at 06.50 it arrives at Hereford at 08.01 and

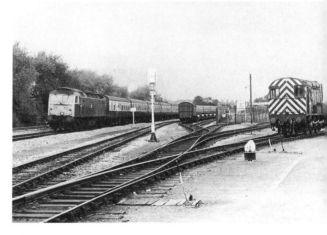

Left:
The only entrance and exit to all three platforms at Oxford is via this small ticket barrier. Oxford became an open station during 1985. *Author*

Top right:
The cramped conditions of the travel centre at Oxford are shown in the above picture. *Author*

Centre right:
Class 50s provide much of the power for the Hereford-Oxford-Paddington services. This picture taken on 24 July 1985 shows No 50003 *Temeraire* leaving Oxford with the 06.00 Hereford-Paddington *Author*

Right:
Oxford South yard is passed by the 14.24 Newcastle-Poole hauled by Class 47/4 No 47440. To the right, pilot No 08946 shunts what is left of the yard here. The two gates in the centre of the picture led to the ex-GWR goods shed, which had been demolished only weeks before this picture was taken. *Author*

immediately forms the 08.05 to Reading via Oxford.

An unusual local working in 1985 was on Sundays when passengers expecting to travel on either the 00.17 all stations to Banbury, or the 01.25 Didcot-Oxford, were surprised to find themselves transported by double-decker buses instead. This novel motive power has been a feature of the local working timetable for quite a few years!

Freight workings today can generally produce daily examples from many of the existing classes of diesel locomotives. Class 20 locomotives now make regular appearances, working in on the 06.05 Bescot-Oxford South yard Speedlink service. They have also appeared on the recently introduced Saltley-Reading crew training run, which arrives at Oxford around midday; Class 45s are also fairly regular visitors on this run. Two other workings of interest, which reach Oxford without actually passing through the station are the FSO 20.10 Llandarcy-Didcot power station oil train; this uses the yard at Hinksey as a locomotive run-round point thus allowing locomotive-first access to Didcot power station. A similar manoeuvre takes place north of Oxford where the 06.53 coal train from Barrow Hill to Bletchington uses Oxford North Junction as a run-round point. Both of these trains are at present rostered for Class 56 locomotives.

Even with the drop in parcels traffic in recent years, Oxford still has its fair share of interesting workings which appear during the hours of darkness. The 23.15 Preston-Reading,

Below:
A Didcot-Barrow Hill empty MGR train moves through Oxford, unusually via the down platform line, hauled by Class 56 No 56095, while Class 37 No 37158 waits to enter the small diesel stabling point here on 26 May 1983.
T. E. J. Waters

Right:
No 47611 *Thames* stands at the up platform with the 06.02 Derby-Brighton on 19 July 1985, as a pair of Class 20s Nos 20004 and 20019 leave for the north after depositing the 06.05 Bescot-Oxford South yard Speedlink service, which can be seen in the background. To the right, a Didcot-Oxford DMU arrives at the down platform. *Author*

Bottom right:
Radley station on a sunny day in 1982, with Class 31 No 31122 on an oil train, bound for Hinksey yard. The car in the background is standing on the site of the Abingdon branch bay. *Author*

the 00.10 Manchester-Crawley new yard and the 03.01 Birmingham-Southampton Western Docks are the pick of the night workings.

Of the two branch lines which survive, the ex-Wycombe Railway line from Kennington Junction to Morris Cowley now sees the most traffic. With Cowley having become the main freight terminal for Oxford, Hinksey once Oxford's largest yard has now become nothing more than a series of exchange sidings, used mainly by trains going either to Cowley or Bicester Ordnance Depot. Once the stronghold of Oxford locomotive crews, Cowley has now been reached by Saltley men, which means that any type of current diesel locomotive may now be seen on the branch. July 1985 saw major track renewal at the Cowley site; many of the 50-year old sidings have been replaced to accommodate the increasing amount of freight traffic which arrives at this large terminal area.

The other local branch still operating is the old Buckinghamshire Railway route from Oxford North Junction to Bletchley. Today there are three regular daily freight workings; the 10.00 Cowley-Bicester COD pick-up freight, the 03.05 Stoke Gifford-Wolverton stone train and the 04.10 Stoke Gifford-Calvert refuse train. Another stone train, the 05.30 Stoke Gifford-Oxford Banbury Road sidings, runs as required.

The greatest local interest, however, stems from the speculation of the possible reinstatement of a passenger service on this line, almost certainly to Bicester, but possibly also as far as the New City of Milton Keynes. To test the ice, so to speak, a special shoppers' train from Oxford was run on 11 May 1985, hauled by No 47618 *Fair Rosamund*; this was certainly deemed a great success by the many passengers who patronised the train. The various local councils have shown an increasing interest in the possible reinstatement of the service and with the help of local pressure groups Oxford may once again have a direct passenger connection to the West Coast main line!

Certainly a weekday at Oxford continues to produce many interesting workings, and with over 200 passenger and freight trains per day, Oxford continues to maintain its interest as a rail centre for both passengers and enthusiasts alike.

In conclusion, a comparison of railways at Oxford during 1958 and 1985 makes interesting reading. In 1958 the staff at Oxford

numbered approximately 1,100, of whom 360 were in the Operating Department, and a further 420 were concerned with locomotive running and maintenance. During a 24hr period some 178 passenger and parcel trains passed through the station; added to this must be 150 goods trains, with most using the local yards which dealt with approximately 2,200 wagons daily.

In 1958, 620,000 passenger tickets were issued at Oxford; the goods department saw 87,000 parcels forwarded and some 320,000 received. Interestingly, at the start of each University term, the station would be inundated by the arrival of about 4,000 trunks and nearly 1,000 bicycles.

By 1985 the staff numbers were reduced to just 209, which includes a total of 51 drivers. The number of parcels and passenger trains passing through each weekday over a 24hr period is about 140. Goods traffic has fallen to just 64 trains per day, a total which includes 17 Merry-go-round workings and 20 Freightliner trains. It must be pointed out, however, that modern-day freight wagons in general carry much greater payloads than wagons did in 1958. Although the figure for parcels handled is not available, the service does currently generate a revenue of approximately £0.2 million per annum. Due to a different method of recording ticket sales precise figures of tickets sold each year are not available, but currently passenger services at Oxford are producing a revenue figure of £5 million per annum. Although the overall figures indicate a reduction in traffic locally compared with 1958, aggressive local marketing in all services is producing a steady growth in traffic and revenue.

Below left:
A pair of Class 37s leave the Bletchley line at Aristotle Lane Junction with the return Wolverton-Stoke Gifford roadstone empties on 12 June 1984. *T. E. J. Waters*

Below:
Hinksey yard in 1984 with a set of MGR wagons bound for Didcot, together with withdrawn Southern Region EMU stock en route to Birds scrapyard, Long Marston for cutting up. This large yard was built during 1942 and was once shunted 24hr per day, but now sadly it is little used and much of the trackwork has been removed, leaving only a few sidings at the north end. It could see a new lease of life if the proposed Parkway station is ever built, as it will stand on this site. *Author*

Top:
The 09.24 Desford Colliery-Didcot MGR speeds through Oxford on 3 June 1985, hauled by Class 58 No 58029. Since the end of the coal strike, Class 58 locomotives form the bulk of the motive power for these trains. Bristol allocated DMU No B427 stands in the old West Midland sidings at the south of the station. *Author*

Above:
Morris Cowley freight depot now forms the terminus of the old Wycombe Railway at the Oxford end. On the evening of 13 June 1985, Class 45 No 45048 waits to despatch its train load of German gearboxes into the nearby Leyland factory. The line in the centre once formed the old 'main line' to Risborough. To the right of the picture stands Cowley Class 08 pilot No 08946. *Author*

The Great Western Locomotive Depots

When the Oxford Railway opened from Didcot during June 1844, locomotives working on the branch were serviced at the Didcot end, where the Great Western Railway had provided a small locomotive shed and turntable. At the Oxford terminus, however, only basic servicing facilities were provided. The water for the locomotives was obtained from the nearby River Thames and was stored within the station area in large barrels until required. These would then have to be manhandled on to the locomotives to fill the water tanks. Coal was stored in hessian sacks and similarly was hand loaded.

It was not until the railway was extended from Millstream Junction to Banbury and Birmingham that proper locomotive servicing facilities were provided at Oxford. In July 1850 a broad gauge shed was built just to the north of the new station site on the up side. Once opened, Didcot lost its locomotive allocation but did continue to be used for occasional servicing. The new broad gauge shed at Oxford measured approximately 230ft × 35ft and was constructed of wood. It contained two running roads and a small workshop area. A small turntable was situated in the yard outside, which also gave access to one of the shed roads. The water supply to the depot was obtained from a well situated at the south end of the up platform. On opening, the depot had an allocation of four locomotives; by 1853 this had risen to eight. The old records show that the highest number of broad gauge locomotives allocated to the depot was 18, this was during the early part of 1861. The influx of standard gauge services to the area in late 1861 signalled the reduction of broad gauge engines at Oxford, and by the beginning of 1863 the allocation had dropped to just seven. This number remained static until November 1868 when the broad gauge track was removed north of Oxford, and by January 1869 only three locomotives were working from the shed. The cessation of broad gauge services at Oxford during 1872 saw the depot close. It continued to be used as a carriage shed until 1879, when it was demolished to allow alterations to the yard.

The Oxford, Worcester & Wolverhampton Railway started running trains into Oxford from June 1853, and very soon built a small engine shed just north of the station at Cripley meadow. This standard gauge shed was duly opened for use during 1854. Early OW&WR records show that four of five engines were working from this shed at the time. This one-road shed was capable of holding six locomotives and, like the Great Western Railway broad gauge depot opposite, was built of wood. A small turntable was provided alongside the shed.

In October 1861 the Great Western Railway started to run standard gauge services from Paddington to Birmingham via Banbury, and to Worcester and Wolverhampton via the West Midland lines. At this time the only standard gauge servicing facilities in the area were provided at the West Midland Railway shed. With this increase in standard gauge traffic, the Great Western Railway was now in need of a site to build a standard gauge locomotive shed. From July 1861 the West Midland and the GWR were unofficially working together, prior to the takeover of the West Midland by the GWR in 1863. This co-operation allowed the Great Western Railway to use the small West Midland site at Oxford for their own locomotive servicing. The facilities very soon proved inadequate, and during 1862 the GWR built a larger four-road wooden shed, incorporating the small single-road West Midland depot. The site was generally remodelled and a larger turntable was installed.

During 1875 a small lifting shop was established which contained a 50-ton lifting crane. A large 24,000gal water tower, supplied from the nearby Thames by pumps situated in the main-shed buildings, was also incorporated into the roof of this building.

In 1908 the down station platform was extended northwards and this meant a new connection had to be provided. This was achieved by adding a span to the river bridge north of the station allowing new access to the extended down bay and the Cripley carriage sidings. To facilitate this, the No 4 road at the shed was shortened by approximately 50ft.

The remainder of the shed building was also refurbished at this time.

The provision, during 1940, of a new junction at Oxford North, between the Great Western Railway lines and the LMS Bletchley line, greatly increased the amount of through traffic using Oxford. This, of course, put a great deal of pressure on the already congested locomotive yard and servicing facilities. Unfortunately, the small corrugated iron coal stage had been constructed well before the advent of the large 4,000gal tenders and did not have the required height to allow locomotives fitted with these to pass under the coaling ramp. A feature therefore of the Oxford

Below:
Locomotive depots at Oxford through the years.

tender locomotives at this time was that they were all fitted with the smaller 3,000 or 3,500gal capacity types.

The situation was resolved in November 1944 when, under the wartime Transport Finance Plan, the small goods yard at Oxford North, adjacent to the locomotive depot, was removed and a new double-sided coaling plant was built on the site; this was now capable of dealing with the largest of locomotives. At the same time the old coal stage was removed, and the entrance and exit to the yard were greatly altered to alleviate congestion. Many extra sidings were provided for locomotive stabling. One of these ran alongside the allotments to the west of the new coaling plant; visiting Midland and Eastern engines would usually be stabled on this line. It was known as 'Tommy

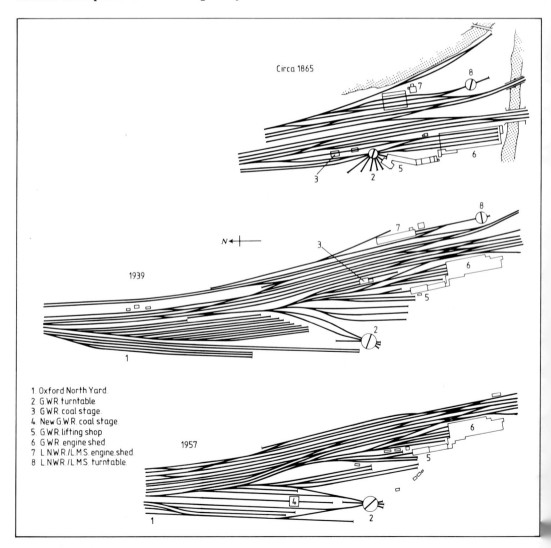

Circa 1865

1939

N

1957

1. Oxford North Yard
2. GWR turntable
3. GWR coal stage
4. New GWR coal stage
5. GWR lifting shop
6. GWR engine shed
7. LNWR/LMS engine shed
8. LNWR/LMS turntable

Above:
This view taken in 1941 shows clearly the locomotive yard at Oxford GWR prior to being remodelled. Just out of picture to the right stands the old coaling stage; to the left is Oxford North yard. *British Rail*

Below:
This fine view shows Oxford locomotive depot yard in July 1965 only six months before closure. The re-roofed depot can be seen in the background with an assortment of locomotives scattered around the coaling plant. *John R. P. Hunt*

Attwood's Siding', apparently after a railwayman who kept an allotment adjacent to this line. This revised layout now allowed incoming locomotives to enter the yard by a new north entrance opposite Oxford North Junction, and outgoing locomotives to leave at the south end by way of a connection almost alongside the steam shed building.

A particularly interesting feature of this new locomotive yard was the provision at the North end of an emergency supply of coal. This lay in massive heaps on both sides of the supply line, with the stock being maintained at several thousand tons. The total cost of the remodelling work was £48,735. Overall, the alterations approximately doubled the size of the locomotive yard complex. The loss of the old Oxford North goods yard was easily absorbed by the new yard that had been built to the south of Oxford at Hinksey during 1942.

An unusual incident occurred on the evening of 5 September 1957, when an ex-LMS 2-8-0 No 48417 of 86G Pontypool Road depot fell into the turntable pit. It had apparently been standing unmanned in light steam alongside the coaling stage with the regulator slightly open. As steam built up the engine moved forward; unfortunately the turntable was wrongly set and the engine fell into the pit. The locomotive was retrieved two days later, but the turntable was out of use until 11 October. During this time locomotives were turned on either the Yarnton turntable or triangle, travelling coupled together four or five at a time to turn. It has always been interesting to speculate that, had the turntable been set correctly, the engine would have ended up in the River Thames alongside, and would have proved a challenging exercise in retrieval.

The new, enlarged yard and increased traffic saw Oxford's locomotive allocation rise from a prewar total of 41 steam locomotives to a total in 1943 of 65, which was surpassed only by the 1959 allocation of 68 steam locomotives. This was the highest number ever allocated at one time to Oxford throughout its entire existence. These balmy days of steam were numbered, however, and the closure of the local branch lines in the early 1960s saw the allocation plummet, and by late 1963 the number stood at just 29 steam locomotives and eight standard 350hp diesel shunters.

To gain extra and more modern office accommodation for the shed staff, the old wooden shed that had stood for over 100 years was partially dismantled in 1963 by removing

the southern end nearest to the river and replacing it with a new flat-roofed, pre-fabricated office building. The northern half of the shed remained, but the whole structure was effectively shortened by about three locomotive lengths.

The remains of the depot continued to be used by both steam locomotives and diesels alike, until the shed officially closed to steam traction at the end of December 1965. However, the shed continued to be used for a few more days, until 3 January 1966, when 'Modified Hall' class 4-6-0 No 6998 *Burton Agnes Hall*, worked out of the depot to haul the last official Western Region steam train to Banbury. Throughout the last five years of its existence as a steam depot, the shedmaster was 'Joe' Trethewey. 'Joe', a Cornishman, started on the GWR in 1935 at St Blazey shed, first as a fireman, and then a driver. GWR also meant 'Go Where Required' and Joe worked over the years at Newton Abbot, Laira and Bristol Bath Road, before becoming shed-

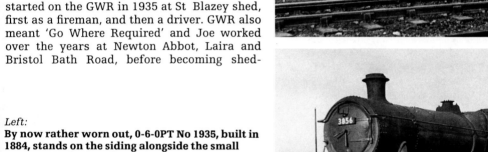

Left:
By now rather worn out, 0-6-0PT No 1935, built in 1884, stands on the siding alongside the small works at Oxford. Built originally as a saddle tank, she was converted to a pannier tank during February 1913. Allocated to Oxford in 1937, she was eventually withdrawn from this shed in November 1953, one of the last survivors of the once numerous '850' class. *G. Hine*

Top right:
This picture, taken in 1947 just prior to Nationalisation, clearly shows the small works and lifting shop at Oxford MPD. The water tank incorporated into the roof is still *in situ* (1986). Also seen in the picture are AEC railcars Nos 10 and 11. *R. H. G. Simpson*

Centre right:
'2884' class 2-8-0 No 3856 stands on the turntable at Oxford shed. The raised area behind the front of the locomotive is the old depot air raid shelter. *Author's collection*

Right:
The small separate lifting shop at Oxford locomotive depot had room for only one engine at a time. Many types of running repairs were carried out in this diminutive building. This picture was taken in 1965 and shows 0-6-0PT No 9773 standing outside the building. No 9773 was the very last locomotive to steam at the shed when, on 4 January 1966, it moved a line of withdrawn locomotives, and then had its own fire dropped for the last time. *Author's collection*

Top:
An excellent view of the inside of Oxford steam shed during the rebuilding of the roof in April 1960. Under normal circumstances this picture would have been almost impossible to take due to the amount of smoke that used to hang around inside the shed. To the left is the stationary washout boiler once carried by an elderly pannier tank, together with 'Hall' class No 5917 *Westminster Hall* and 'Castle' No 7008 *Swansea Castle*. *J. D. Edwards*

Above:
On the morning of 5 September 1957 ex-LMS Stanier '8F' 2-8-0 No 48417 of Pontypool Road depot fell into the turntable pit at Oxford. The above picture shows the locomotive being lifted from the pit on 7 September. The turntable was out of action until repairs were completed on 11 October; locomotives were turned using the Yarnton turntable or triangle during that period. *D. Pye*

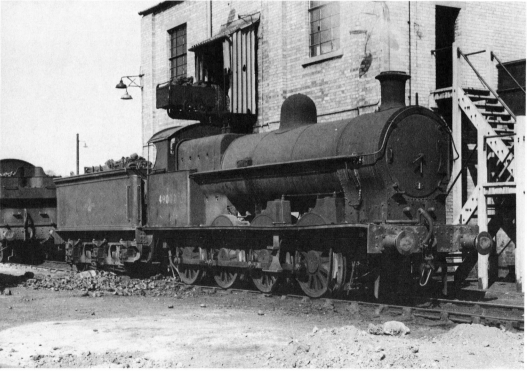

Top:
This fine study shows ex-LNER Class B12 4-6-0 No 61580 preparing to use the turntable prior to working the 2.28pm Oxford-Cambridge train, on 4 May 1958. *J. D. Edwards*

Above:
Ex-LNWR 'G2' 0-8-0 No 49002 of Nuneaton shed stands at the coaling plant at Oxford. These engines were daily visitors to Oxford for many years, working in with freights from the Bletchley line. *J. D. Edwards*

Top:
**Rebuilt Bulleid 'West Country' Pacific No 34042
Dorchester alongside the coaling plant at Oxford
in May 1960.** *Author*

Above:
**Steam has gone, and this 1966 view of the former
GWR shed at Oxford shows complete
dieselisation, with Beyer Peacock Type 3
'Hymeks', an NBL Type 2 and a line of standard
350hp diesel shunters in residence.**
R. H. G. Simpson

Right:
**Taken on 4 November 1957, this photograph
shows a typical daily scene at the locomotive
yard at Oxford. Ex-LNWR 'G2' 0-8-0 No 49061,
ex-SR 'Lord Nelson' class 4-6-0 No 30865 *Sir John
Hawkins* and ex-GWR 0-4-2T No 5818 congregate
around the coaling plant.** *J. D. Edwards*

master at Machynlleth in North Wales during the 1950s. He applied for and obtained the post of shedmaster at Oxford in 1960 and had the sorry task of running this fine old shed during the run-down of steam on the Western Region. When the shed closed he had the distinction of being the very last ex-GW shedmaster at an ex-GW shed. Once closed the shed, turntable and coaling plant were soon removed and the site generally cleared to provide space for a small diesel servicing depot and new carriage sidings which were completed during 1968.

Interestingly, when the roof of the steam depot was removed during demolition, the contractors discovered the original building date, 1862, clearly stamped into the wood of the main supporting cross beam. The small stabling point on the site of the old shed continued to be used for locomotive refuelling until August 1984 when this function was moved to Reading. Oxford locomotive depot, small though it was, closed and locomotive servicing which had taken place on the site for 130 years finally came to an end.

Traces of the days of steam are still visible, however. At the time of writing the water tower which had formed part of the old lifting shop is still *in situ*; also the brick foundation wall of the original small OW&WR shed which was incorporated into the Great Western Railway depot in 1862 is still clearly visible alongside the main line. Locomotives continue to be stabled on this site, so for the time being at least, part of the tradition is still in existence.

Throughout the years the GWR employed large numbers of men at the steam depot, but the numbers surprisingly reached an all-time high during the 1950s when 435 men were employed at the depot. Of these, 280 were drivers and firemen, the balance being made up of maintenance and shed staff. The removal of steam traction during the 1960s, together with the closure of many lines, saw a continuous reduction in staffing levels until at the time of writing (1985) only 51 drivers are required at Oxford, with an ancillary staff of about 20.

Top:
The small retaining wall of the original OW&WR single road engine shed at Oxford. This is now the only visible evidence of the steam depot removed during early 1968. *Author*

Above:
The small refuelling bay and stabling point at Oxford on the site of the old steam depot. The refuelling bay is now closed and few locomotives stable at Oxford today. Here in 1983, Classes 47, 31, 50, 40, 56 and 08 are in evidence. The large water tower is all that remains of the steam lifting shop. *Brian Daniels*

Motive Power Summary

From the earliest days of railway operation in Oxford there has always been a varied selection of motive power for working the many services in the area.

On the opening of the Oxford Railway in 1844 the GW provided a motley selection of broad gauge locomotives for the new services. The two Haigh Foundry engines *Snake* and *Viper* were probably some of the first engines on the branch and were certainly still working in the area during 1846. Other locomotives working into Oxford at this time included examples of both 'Star' and 'Firefly' 2-2-2 classes.

The extension of the line to Banbury and beyond in 1850 saw the requirement for more powerful locomotives, and when the broad gauge depot opened at Oxford, examples of the 'Priam', 'Abbot' and 'Leo' classes were allocated here but were very soon replaced by the larger 8ft single 'Iron Duke' class of engine, which from 1856 formed the bulk of the Oxford passenger allocation. Engines of the 'Fury' and 'Caesar' classes were provided for the goods services. The introduction of standard gauge services in 1861 saw the gradual demise of broad gauge working in the area until it was removed completely in 1872.

The opening by the GWR of the standard gauge engine shed at Cripley Meadow in 1862 brought the first official standard gauge allocation to Oxford. Many of the workings now passed into the hands of Gooch-designed engines, Nos 69-76 built by Beyer Peacock between 1855 and 1856 were at Oxford for working the first standard gauge trains. These 2-2-2s were rebuilt during the 1890s as 2-4-0s becoming the 'River' class; they were all still working from Oxford during 1901. Other early allocations included some of the 'Sharps' of 1862, and the 'Sir Daniel' class 2-2-2 locomotives. From the mid-1860s until the turn of the century 'Queen' class, 'Cobhams', '517s', and 'Metro' tanks formed the bulk of the allocation.

The opening of the connection from the GC at Banbury Junction in 1900 saw an increase of through workings, and to cope with this extra traffic Oxford gained many 'Barnham'

class 2-4-0s. Between 1907 and 1912 Oxford had a small allocation of 'Achilles' class 4-2-2 locomotives for use on the intermediate services. Fine though these engines were, by the time they arrived at Oxford they were well past their best.

By the start of World War 1, many of the older locomotives had disappeared from the area but the allocation still contained many '517', 'Metro' and 0-6-0 tanks with 'Bulldog' and 'City' class 4-4-0s for the main line turns, supplemented by the three French compounds, *La France*, *President* and *Alliance* which arrived during 1915.

1920 saw the first allocation to Oxford of five examples of the Churchward 'Saint' class 4-6-0 but these left the area during 1922 and were replaced by more 'Citys', which together with the 'Atbara' and 'Flower' class engines provided Oxford with a very strong 4-4-0 allocation which lasted throughout the rest of the decade.

Below:
This excellent picture shows 'Cobham' class 2-2-2 No 165, built in 1879, outside the wooden GWR depot at Oxford. The locomotive was the very last example of this handsome class, being withdrawn from Oxford in December 1914 just six months after the picture was taken.
Ken Nunn collection courtesy LCGB

Top:
For a good number of years until 1920 the 2-4-0 'Barnhams' worked many of the secondary trains around the Oxford area. Numerous members of the class were allocated to Oxford for these workings. This particular one, No 3211, built in 1889, was allocated here from 1917 until 1920 when all of this class were transferred away. *L&GRP (14090)*

Above:
Probably one of the most famous tank engines of all time was '517' class 0-4-2T No 1473, *Fair Rosamund*, shown here at Oxford in 1920, prior to being rebuilt with an enclosed cab. Named in 1896 for working a royal train to Blenheim, this engine worked mainly on the Woodstock branch from 1896 until its withdrawal in 1935. It is rumoured that one of the wooden and brass nameplates still survives somewhere in the Woodstock area. *L&GRP (14085)*

The 1930s saw the arrival of a batch of worn-out 'County' class 4-4-0 engines — never a favourite with Oxford men. They were all withdrawn by 1933 and replaced by examples of the newly built 'Hall' class 4-6-0; the first of which, No 4957 *Postlip Hall*, arrived in February 1931. This brought a certain degree of standardisation to the Oxford allocation, which was to remain until the end of the steam era. The influx of 'Halls' increased during the decade, and by 1938 there were 11 examples working from Oxford. The secondary and branch workings were now in the hands of 0-6-0 pannier tanks, Metro 2-4-0T and 61XX 2-6-2T locomotives. The ageing '517' class 0-4-2T was replaced in 1935 by examples of the newly-constructed '4800' class 0-4-2T. The

same year Oxford also gained two of the new GWR diesel railcars. Goods traffic was now handled by '28XX' 2-8-0, 'Aberdare' 2-6-0 and 'Dean Goods' 0-6-0 engines. This decade also saw the arrival of 4-6-0s of the four-cylinder 'Star' class for fast services.

The advent of World War 2 brought many alterations in the area, and with new junctions and yards being provided locally, the subsequent increase in traffic reflected itself on the locomotive scene, with examples of LMS classes and United States Army Transportation Corps 2-8-0 engines being allocated to Oxford. During 1942 nine new '38XXs' also arrived to cater for the wartime goods traffic. The end of the war saw only a slight reduction in the total allocation.

Above:
Locomotive No 3702 *Halifax* built in 1901, a Dean-designed 'City' class 4-4-0, seen at Oxford in 1920. This engine was allocated here from early 1913 until late 1927, and, together with several other members of the class worked fast and semi-fast trains to Worcester, Birmingham and London. The picture also shows the small corrugated iron coaling plant at Oxford which was demolished in 1945. *L&GRP (14095)*

Right:
'Aberdare' class 2-6-0 No 2670 approaches Oxford on 15 February 1930 with an up goods. Note the two LMS four-wheel wagons next to the locomotive. *OURS collection*

Milestones were passed in 1947 with the withdrawal of No 1159, the last of the '517' tanks, and in 1949 with the end of No 3588, the very last 'Metro'. However, this latter year also saw the arrival of two brand new 'Castle' class locomotives, Nos 7008 *Swansea Castle* and 7010 *Avondale Castle* which replaced 'Stars' Nos 4049 *Princess Maud* and 4052 *Princess Beatrice*. Luckily No 4021 *British Monarch* survived for another three years; it had been an Oxford engine since 1937. During 1948 two '45XX' 2-6-2Ts arrived for working on the Fairford Branch. 1950 opened with the allocation standing at 54 steam locomotives and one diesel railcar. During the year 0-6-0PT No 1742 was withdrawn, the last example of the '655' class at Oxford. Throughout the remainder of

Right:
The Michelin railcar entering the up platform at Oxford GWR, the occasion being a demonstration run to Reading on 24 April 1932, when free tickets were issued for the trip. The small size of this vehicle is most apparent against the standard-height platform facing.
Courtesy OURS

Below:
Looking south from Wolvercot Junction 'Hall' No 5995 *Wick Hall* on the Bournemouth-Newcastle through train passes a goods hauled by '2800' Class No 2853. At this same point today the view is bisected by the Oxford ring road.
J. D. Edwards

Bottom right:
Diesel railcar No 12, built by the Gloucester Railway Carriage & Wagon Co in 1936 for the GWR, stands alongside the railcar refuelling point at Oxford MPD. These machines regularly worked on the Risborough and Witney branches. This railcar was allocated to Oxford from 1954 until its withdrawal in 1957.
Real Photographs (K2106)

the 1950s the main services were handled by three 'Castles' and 14 'Halls' with the addition of some 'Grange' class 4-6-0s from 1956. Surprisingly 1959 saw the highest number of locomotives ever allocated to Oxford — 68, all steam. The last ex-GWR diesel railcars at Oxford had been withdrawn during 1957.

The rundown of the services, with the closure of the local branch lines in the early 1960s saw the allocation plummet, and by 1964 just a few pannier and prairie tanks, together with various 'Halls' and 'Granges' remained. Oxford was the last of the ex-GWR steam depots to remain open on the Western Region, so it became the dumping ground for redundant locomotives from other depots. Although the official allocation was now down to below 30, the actual number on shed at any time during the last couple of years rarely fell below 50.

Apart from the wide variety of Great Western locomotive types that could be seen at Oxford, it was the daily appearances of locomotives from each of the other regions that made Oxford such a mecca for railway enthusiasts during the days of steam. The LNWR and later the LMS were always well represented over the years with the many workings into Rewley Road, and the various

types of locomotives are described in the chapter on this line.

During the latter part of the 19th century, LSWR locomotives were frequent visitors to Oxford, many working in on goods trains. The through Southampton-Oxford passenger service was at this time regularly worked by various Drummond 4-4-0 types. The inauguration of the through Bournemouth, Sheffield and Newcastle services early this century increased the daily frequency of LSWR engines working into Oxford with the down portions of these trains. Right up until the end of World War 2 it was possible to see ex-LSWR 'L12', 'T9' and the ever popular 'King Arthur' class engines working in on these Bournemouth trains. The mid-1950s, however, saw the decline of the 'Arthurs', being replaced by either 'Lord Nelsons' or the newer Bulleid Pacifics; the latter types were to work on this service until the end of steam locally.

The Great Central and North Eastern engines on the up portion of these trains were usually changed at Banbury, but quite often would work right through, to effect the change at Oxford. This situation regularly brought GC Class B3, B4, B7 and B8 locomotives into the city with just the occasional 'C1' and 'C4' Atlantics and Class B17 'Sandringhams'. Loco-

Top:
Brown-Boveri gas turbine locomotive No 18000 on a test train at Oxford on 24 April 1950, one month before being officially accepted into stock by the Western Region. This locomotive was built in Switzerland for the Western Region and ran in this country until withdrawn in December 1960. *R. H. G. Simpson*

Above:
Unrebuilt Bulleid Pacific No 34102 *Lapford* leaves Oxford with the southbound 'Pines Express' on 28 February 1963. This train was re-routed via Oxford and Reading from September 1962.
Dr G. Smith

Top:
Two rebuilt Bulleid Pacifics pass at Oxford on 8 August 1964. 'Merchant Navy' No 35021 *New Zealand Line* is about to leave with the southbound 'Pines Express' as 'West Country' No 34097 *Holsworthy* enters the station with a Poole-Sheffield service. *S. Creer*

Above:
Ex-GCR Class B8 4-6-0 No 5446 stands at the up platform at Oxford with the 9.20am from Sheffield to Swansea, on 31 March 1946. The locomotive will work right through to Swindon. *R. H. G. Simpson*

Backing out of the up bay after arriving from Cambridge is Gresley 'K3' 2-6-0 No 61834. These engines were regular visitors to Oxford, working in on parcel trains via Bedford and Bletchley. Author's collection

Left:
Ex-LNER Class B12 No 61546 waits, unusually at the down platform, with the 2.28pm to Cambridge on 23 April 1959. It was usual for this service to use the down bay. J. D. Edwards

Above:
Fowler 'Crab' 2-6-0 No 42859 moves a mixed goods from the Midlands through Oxford station and onwards to Hinksey yard on a sunny afternoon in 1961. S. Boorne

motives from these classes were also regularly seen on the evening Hull-Swindon fish trains and the Sundays only Sheffield-Swansea passenger service, working through as far as Swindon. During the years after the war, engines of the 'B1', 'K3' and 'V2' classes were to monopolise all of these services.

The running of through passenger and parcel trains from Cambridge brought locomotives of yet another company into Oxford on a daily basis; 'B12' and 'D16' types of the Great Eastern Railway regularly worked these trains with occasional 0-6-0s of Classes J19 and J37. Once again these were replaced in the late 1950s by examples of Classes B1 and K3.

Apart from the Bletchley and Bedford passenger services, many of the ex-LNWR and LMS locomotives came into Oxford with goods trains. Many of course worked into Rewley Road yard, and after 1940 through Oxford via North Junction. This route brought the LMS '4F', 'Crab', Class 5 and '8F' types, with of course the ex-LNWR Class G1 and G2 0-8-0s through to the various yards locally. Surprisingly enough, almost as many arrived from the Birmingham area via the GWR main line. Regular daily Crewe, Saltley and Nuneaton workings brought many of the above classes into the city via this route with the interesting additions of 'Patriot', 'Jubilee' and 'Royal Scot' types, many of which appeared on the daily Morris Cowley-Washwood Heath car trains.

The end of steam locally in 1966 brought an end to this wide variety of locomotive types, from each of the 'Big Four' companies, which had been synonymous with railway working in Oxford since the turn of the century.

Steam traction finally came to an end at Oxford on 3 January 1966 when 'Modified Hall' No 6998 *Burton Agnes Hall* worked the 2.20pm to Newcastle as far as Banbury. The Lady Mayoress of Oxford, Mrs Catherine Lower, was on the footplate as the locomotive left the shed and moved to its train at the platform. The engine had been fitted earlier in the day with a set of replica nameplates made especially for the occasion by boilersmith Len Cross. The departure of *Burton Agnes Hall* ended 122 years of GW steam traction at Oxford. Luckily the locomotive has been saved and is now only 10 miles away at the Great Western Society's depot at Didcot, along with other preserved ex-GW locomotives.

Well before this date many of the trains at Oxford were being diesel hauled. The through workings from the North to the south coast started to produce Brush Type 4 (Class 47) workings. The 'Castles' and 'Halls' on the

Left:
In early blue livery with yellow warning panels, Beyer Peacock 'Hymek' No D7034 brings a lengthy up freight through Oxford in April 1968. *David Birch*

Below:
Looking north from the A423 road bridge at Kidlington on 19 April 1968, English Electric Type 4 No D334 with a train of empty bogie flats passes the small signalbox at Kidlington. The goods loop to the left of the picture was once the line from Kidlington station to Woodstock. Today not only has the loop been removed, together with the signalbox and semaphore signals, but the locomotive also has passed into history. *S. Boorne*

Worcester trains gave way to 'Hymek' and 'Warship' class diesel-hydraulics, with the occasional 'Western' class locomotive (Class 52) filling in, and from the start of 1966 these four classes of diesel became responsible for hauling almost all of the passenger traffic through Oxford. Diesel multiple-units had started to appear on semi-fast services as early as 1958, very rapidly displacing steam from these workings. During the 1960s and early 1970s, the 'Hymeks', 'Warships' and 'Westerns' were gradually withdrawn by the Western Region, with the services producing more and more Class 47 workings. The arrival of the Class 50s from the London Midland Region during the mid-1970s has seen these locomotives establish themselves on many workings.

Locomotive-hauled passenger services in 1986 are in the hands of just two types of diesel. The through InterCity services from the south coast to the North are almost exclusively hauled by Class 47 locomotives, examples turning up from most depots, including those in Scotland. The Worcester services together with the Oxford-Paddington trains are mostly Class 50 hauled with some Class 47s also appearing. Just occasionally a Class 45 or 33 will turn up on the afternoon Portsmouth-Birmingham, a train that on one occasion produced double-headed Class 73s. Members of Class 31 also sometimes deputise on passenger services.

Freight traffic, however, still provides a good variation of locomotive types, Local trip freights, newspaper trains and some car traffic produce Classes 20, 25, 31, 47 and 50. The MGR coal traffic is now handled by Classes 47 and 58 from Toton depot, with some Class 56 locomotives still appearing on the Barrow Hill trains. The roadstone traffic still produces double-headed Class 37s but is mainly hauled by Bristol-allocated Class 56 engines. All in all, Oxford still has plenty to interest the enthusiast.

Below:
Class 43 'Warship' No D851 *Temeraire* in almost ex-works condition stands in the summer sun at Shipton-on-Cherwell cement works sidings, with the local Oxford-Banbury pick up freight in July 1968. Powered by two MAN engines, this 2,200hp Type 4 locomotive was built by North British in 1961 and withdrawn just 10 years later in May 1971. *D. Parker*

Locomotive Allocations

Last Survivors

During the latter years of steam traction on the Western Region, many withdrawals meant that the last remnants of a once fine steam locomotive fleet were being dumped at Oxford. It was in the early years before, and just after both World Wars, that Oxford became the final working depot for many old GW locomotive types, some of which are listed below. Due to lack of official records, individual locomotives working from Oxford prior to 1901 are difficult to trace. The locomotives listed below were all the last survivors of their respective classes.

No	Class	Built	Withdrawn
10	'Royal Albert' (Experimental class rebuilt in 1890 as 2-2-2 7ft 0in single)	June 1886	January 1906
104	*Alliance* De Glehn Compound 4-4-2	June 1905	September 1928
113	'111' class 2-4-0	December 1863	April 1914
157	'157' class 2-2-2 of 1862	April 1862	September 1881
165	'Cobham' class 2-2-2	November 1879	December 1914
1128	*Duke of York* 'Queen' class 2-2-2	June 1875	April 1914
1159	'517' class 0-4-2T	January 1876	August 1947
3588	'Metro' class 2-4-0T	August 1899	December 1949

Broad Gauge
Locomotive Allocations

December 1855
Passenger Engines
2-2-2 'Priam' class: *Achilles, Electra, Erebus, Harpy, Hector, Queen, Tiger*
4-2-2 'Iron Duke' class: *Perseus, Swallow*
4-4-0 'Abbot' class: *Pirate*
Goods Engines
0-6-0 'Caesar' class: *Cyprus, Florence, Isis, Thunderer*
2-4-0 'Leo' class: *Dromedary*
Ballast Engine
0-6-0 'Premier' class: *Premier*
TOTAL: 16

March 1861
Passenger Engines
4-2-2 'Iron Duke' class: *Amazon, Crimea, Estaffete, Eupatoria, Perseus, Rover, Rougemont, Warlock*
Goods Engines
0-6-0 'Caesar' class: *Cambyses, Gyfeillon, Hebe, Janus, Monarch, Nemesis, Nimrod, Typhon*
2-4-0 'Leo' class: *Hella*

2-2-2 'Priam' class: *Panther*
TOTAL: 18

In 1860 the broad gauge allocation at Oxford was distributed as follows:
Passenger Workings 6
Abingdon 1
Didcot Goods 6
Pilot 1

Right:
Between 1903 and 1905 the GWR purchased three De Glehn compound 4-4-2 locomotives from the Société Alsacienne de Constructions Mécaniques of Belfort, France. These locomotives were known to GWR men as 'the Frenchmen' and from 1915 were allocated to Oxford, where they worked fast and semi-fast trains to Paddington and Birmingham. No 104 *Alliance*, shown here at Oxford MPD in 1920, was withdrawn in 1928. No 102 *La France* lasted until 1926, and No 103 *President* until 1927. All three were allocated to Oxford at the time of withdrawal.
L&GRP (14092)

Oxford GWR Allocation January 1901

2-2-2 'Cobham' class
157
159

2-2-2 'Sir Daniel' class
480
577
578

4-2-2 'Achilles' class
3005 *Britannia*

2-4-0 'River' class
69 *Avon*
70 *Dart*
71 *Dee*
72 *Exe*
73 *Isis*
74 *Stour*

2-4-0 '481' class
487

2-4-0 '2201' class
2210

2-4-0 'Barnham' class
3217

4-4-0 'Bulldog' class
3345 *Perseus*
3358 *Godolphin*

0-6-0 'Standard Goods'
23
788
799
1186

0-6-0 'Dean Goods'
2325
2337
2357
2387
2397
2400
2457
2499

0-6-0 '2361' class
2374

2378

0-4-2T '517' class
520

2-4-0T 'Metropolitan' class
455

4-4-0T Ex-Monmouth Railway & Canal Co
1306

0-6-0ST '1016' class
1033

0-6-0ST '850' class
1927
1993

0-6-0ST '1661' class
1690
1699

0-6-0ST '1854' class
1859
1866
1867

Locomotives outstabled
ABINGDON:
0-4-2T '517' class
564
1425

FAIRFORD:
2-2-2 'Sir Daniel' class
379

WOODSTOCK:
0-4-2T '517' class
1473 *Fair Rosamund*

CHIPPING NORTON
    JUNCTION:
0-6-0ST '1854' class
1861

Total: 47

Oxford GWR Allocation January 1930

4-4-0 'Bulldog' class
3356 *Sir Stafford*

4-4-0 'County' class
3803 *County Cork*
3804 *County Dublin*
3811 *County of Bucks*
3814 *County of Chester*
3821 *County of Bedford*
3826 *County of Flint*
3827 *County of Gloucester*
3829 *County of Merioneth*
3832 *County of Wilts*
3835 *County of Devon*

4-4-0 'Badminton' class
4101 *Barrington*
4113 *Samson*

0-6-0 'Dean Goods'
2344
2429

2-6-0 'Aberdare' class
2646

4-6-0 'Saint' class
2902 *Lady of the Lake*
2920 *Saint David*

2-8-0 '2800' class
2863

0-4-2T '517' class
1466
1473 *Fair Rosamund*

2-4-0T 'Metropolitan' class
457
626
1413
1492
1498

0-6-0PT '1016' class
1026

0-6-0PT '1076' class
1134
1294
1569

0-6-0PT '1661' class
1688

0-6-0PT '1854' class
1898

0-6-0PT '850' class
1935
1976

2-6-2T '5100' class
5123
5133

Total: 36

Oxford GWR Allocation 1943

0-6-0 '2251' class
2240

0-6-0 '2301' class
2395

2-6-0 '4300' class
6359
9303
9316
9317

4-6-0 'Star' class
4004 *Morning Star*
4021 *British Monarch*

4052 *Princess Beatrice*

4-6-0 'Hall' class
4902 *Aldenham Hall*
4903 *Astley Hall*
4921 *Eaton Hall*
4922 *Enville Hall*
4928 *Gatacre Hall*
4938 *Liddington Hall*
4973 *Sweeney Hall*
5904 *Kelham Hall*
5960 *St Edmund Hall*
6925 *Hackness Hall*
6933 *Birtles Hall*
6937 *Conyngham Hall*

2-8-0 '2800' class
2861
3835
3836
3837
3838
3847
3848
3862
3865

0-4-2T '517' class
1159

0-4-2T '4800' class
4843
4848
4850

2-4-0T '3500' class
3564
3568
3583
3588
3589

0-6-0PT '1501' class
1531

0-6-0PT '655' class
1743

0-6-0PT '1901' class
2007

0-6-0PT '5700' class
3608
3687
3715
3722
3741
3781

3798
4645

0-6-0PT '5400' class
5418

2-6-2T '6100' class
6103
6122
6138

GWR Diesel Railcars
W9
W10
W13

Non-GWR Locomotives
0-6-0 LMS Class 2F
3027
3109
3372

2-8-0 USATC 'S160' class
Alco
1663
2102
2103

Lima
1880
1891
1897

Note:
Alco American Locomotive Co
Lima Lima Locomotive Co

Total: 66

Oxford Depot
26 December 1965

**During Last Week of Steam
Operation**

LOCOMOTIVES IN STEAM
Ex-GWR Locomotives
4-6-0 'Hall' class
5956 *Mottram Hall*

4-6-0 'Modified Hall' class
6991 *Acton Burnell Hall*
6998 *Burton Agnes Hall*
6999 *Capel Dewi Hall*

4-6-0PT '5700' class
4667
4773

2-6-2T '6100' class
6111
6126
6134
6136
6161

Ex-LMS Locomotives
4-6-0 Class 5
44710
44805
45033
45331
45349

2-8-0 Class 8F
48367
48527
48655

*British Railways Standard
Classes*
2-6-0 Class 4
76063

4-6-0 Class 5
73003
73020
73029
73119

2-10-0 Class 9F
92162

Total: 25

DIESEL LOCOMOTIVES
B-B Type 3 'Hymek'
D7058

Co-Co Type 4 Brush
D1596
D1600
D1652
D1747
D1919
D1966

1Co-Co1 Type 4 'Peak'
D118

0-6-0DE 350hp shunter
D3949
D3959
D3960
D3967
D3971

Total: 13

LOCOMOTIVES STORED
UNSERVICEABLE
Ex-GWR Locomotives

4-6-0 'Grange' class
6815 *Frilford Grange*
6847 *Tidmarsh Grange*
6868 *Penrhos Grange*

4-6-0 'Hall' class
4920 *Dumbleton Hall*
4962 *Ragley Hall*
6910 *Gossington Hall*
6921 *Borwick Hall*
6927 *Lilford Hall*
6931 *Aldborough Hall*
6932 *Burwarton Hall*
6944 *Fledborough Hall*
6947 *Helmingham Hall*
6957 *Norcliffe Hall*

4-6-0 'Modified Hall' class
6959 *Peatling Hall*
6967 *Willesley Hall*
6984 *Owsden Hall*
6990 *Witherslack Hall*
6993 *Arthog Hall*
7904 *Fountains Hall*
7907 *Hart Hall*
7909 *Heveningham Hall*
7914 *Lleweni Hall*
7927 *Willington Hall*

0-6-0PT '5700' class
9789

2-6-2T '6100' class
6139

Ex-LMS Locomotives
4-6-0 Class 5
45006

*British Railways Standard
and Austerity Locomotives*

4-6-0 Class 5
73166

2-8-0 Austerity (WD)
90258

2-10-0 Class 9F
92216
92235

Total: 30

Appendices

Scheduled Merry-go-round Coal Trains to Didcot Power Station 1986

Reporting number	Train	Oxford	Runs
7V95	21.53 Bescot up yard-Didcot	23.48	MX
7V51	21.12 Barrow Hill SS-Didcot	00.59	MX
7V20	20.30 Bagworth-Didcot	02.50	MX
7V03	00.44 Baddesley Colliery-Didcot	03.37	MX
7V22	02.40 Barrow Hill SS-Didcot	06.18	MX
7V46	07.02 Toton Old Bank-Didcot	10.38	SX
7V44	09.34 Three Spires Junction-Didcot	11.39	SX
7V54	09.24 Desford Colliery-Didcot	13.01	SX
7V57	09.40 Barrow Hill SS-Didcot	13.45	SX
7V63	11.14 Baddesley Colliery-Didcot	14.21	SX
7V65	11.56 Desford Colliery-Didcot	15.38	SX
7V85	14.01 Toton Old Bank-Didcot	17.34	SX
7V07	13.57 Barrow Hill SS-Didcot	18.06	SX
7V02	14.26 Bagworth-Didcot	19.38	SX
7V60	16.40 Birch Coppice Colliery-Didcot	20.31	SX
7V90	19.55 Three Spires Junction-Didcot	21.55	SX
7V19	18.27 Barrow Hill SS-Didcot	22.51	SX

Note:
Prior to the coal strike of 1984/85 these working were hauled by Class 47 and 56 locomotives. When the strike ended and the services recommenced in March 1985, the bulk of the coal traffic was handled by the new Class 58 locomotives, with only the Barrow Hill workings still producing members of Class 56.

Up Freight Workings through Oxford 1986 excluding MGR Trains

Reporting number	Train	Oxford	Runs
4E34	00.05 Washwood-Harwich	01.41	MX
4067	21.29 Trafford Park-Southampton	01.48	MX
4065	19.53 Trafford Park-Millbrook	03.01	MX
6049	16.05 Haverton Hill-Eastleigh	04.04	MX
4071	22.52 Kingmoor-Southampton	04.56	MO
4073	03.48 Lawley St-Southampton	06.03	MX
6V19	06.05 Bescot-Oxford South Yard	08.42	SX
4V16	09.33 Washwood-Cowley	11.12	SX
6V11	10.03 Wolverton-Stoke Gifford	11.44	SX
4081	03.00 Coatbridge-Southampton	11.50	MX

3V30	06.53 Barrow Hill-Bletchingdon	11.59B	WO
5V04	12.30 Calvert-Bath	13.50	SX
5A02	14.43 Banbury Rd-Stoke Gifford	14.58	SX
6040	12.00 Handsworth-Northfleet	15.16	ThO
4090	12.25 Lawley St-Southampton	17.51	SO
4095	12.15 Aintree-Southampton	18.38	SO
5V36	16.00 Longbridge-Cowley	18.47	SX
4094	15.54 Trafford Park-Southampton	20.19	SO
4095	14.54 Aintree-Southampton	20.28	SX
4E32	20.00 Cowley-Parkeston	20.40H	SX
4096	16.09 Leeds-Southampton	21.18	SO
6043	21.55 Cowley-Dover	22.25H	SX
4062	18.35 Leeds-Southampton	23.18	SX
6032	20.15 Longport-Fawley	23.31	TThO

Notes:

B   Bletchingdon.

H   Hinksey.

Down Freight Workings through Oxford 1986
excluding MGR Trains

Reporting number	Train	Oxford	Runs
4M88	21.54 Southampton-Aintree	00.26	MX
4M57	23.05 Southampton-Trafford Park	01.39	MX
4M58	00.20 Southampton-Trafford Park	02.49	MO
7V27	22.35 Dover Town-Hinksey	04.00H	MX
6M37	04.00 Cowley-Longbridge	04.15	SX
6E76	02.10 Southampton-Leeds	04.43	
6M43	23.50 Parkeston-Washwood	04.53	MX
6M20	03.05 Stoke Gifford-Wolverton	05.11	SX
8337	00.35 Margam-Hinksey	05.20H	MO
6M63	04.10 Stoke Gifford-Calvert	05.57	MX
7709	01.47 Parkeston-Hinksey	06.02	MX
7A04	05.30 Stoke Gifford-Oxford, Banbury Rd Sidings	07.34	SX
6M46	05.00 Northfleet BC1-Greaves	08.25	TThFO
6S59	10.18 Southampton-Coatbridge	13.07	SX
6E01	13.00 Bletchingdon-Barrow Hill	13.42N	WO
6M23	10.12 Fawley-Longport	14.24	TThO
6M60	12.20 Southampton-Lawley St	14.57	SO
6M93	16.20 Cowley-Bescot	16.34	SX
6M59	16.08 Southampton-Kingmoor	18.49	SO
6M79	16.08 Southampton-Lawley Street	18.49	SX
6E30	17.19 Eastleigh-York Dringhouses	20.13	SX
6S64	21.00 Cowley-Bathgate	21.17	SX
6M68	20.40 Millbrook-Trafford Park	23.13	SX

Notes:

H   Hinksey.

N   Oxford North Junction.

Refuge Sidings and Loops

Location	Refuge sidings	Running loops	Wagon capacity
DOWN			
Didcot North Junction-Appleford Crossing	—	1	157
Radley-Sandford	—	1	245
Sandford-Kennington Junction	—	1	285
Kennington Junction	—	1	66
Kennington Junction-Hinksey South	—	1	87
Hinksey South-Hinksey GF	—	1	135
Hinksey GF-Hinksey North	—	1	135
Oxford	—	1	71
Oxford North Junction-Wolvercot Junction	—	1	455
Kidlington	—	1	67
UP			
Kidlington	1	—	58
Wolvercot Junction	—	1	333
Oxford	—	1	65
Hinksey North-Hinksey South	—	1	229
	—	1	173
Hinksey South-Kennington Junction	—	1	109
Kennington Junction	1	—	58
Sandford-Radley	—	1	250
Appleford Crossing-Didcot North Junction	—	1	157

Note:
The above list shows refuge sidings and goods loops situated in the Oxford area in 1958. Many o
these had been installed during World War 2 to accommodate the vastly increased traffic i
Oxfordshire. Almost all had been removed by 1985.

Signalboxes in the Oxford Area in 1948

Main Line

Didcot North Junction
Appleford Crossing
Culham
Nuneham
Radley
Sandford
Kennington Junction
Hinksey South
Hinksey North
Oxford Station South
Oxford Station North
Oxford North Junction
Wolvercot Siding
Wolvercot Junction
Kidlington

Branch Lines

Abingdon Branch
Abingdon

Witney Branch
Yarnton Junction
Eynsham
Witney Station
Brize Norton and Bampton
Carterton
Lechlade
Fairford

Princes Risborough Line
Thame
Wheatley
Morris Cowley

LNWR Bletchley Line
Rewley Road
Port Meadow
Oxford Banbury Road Junction
Islip
Bicester

Dates of Opening

Date	Company	Section	Gauge
2 June 1844	Oxford Railway Co	Didcot Junction, Oxford	Broad
2 September 1850	Great Western Railway	Oxford Millstream Junction-Banbury	Broad, single line
0 May 1851	Buckinghamshire Railway/London & North Western	Bletchley-Oxford Rewley Road	Standard
1 October 1852	Great Western Railway	Oxford Millstream Junction-Birmingham	Mixed, double track
4 June 1853	Oxford Worcester & Wolverhampton Railway	Evesham-Wolvercot Junction	Part mixed, broad gauge not used
2 June 1856	Abingdon Railway Co	Abingdon Junction-Abingdon	Broad
2 December 1856	Great Western Railway	Oxford Isis Bridge-Didcot	Mixed
4 November 1861	Witney Railway	Yarnton Junction-Witney	Standard
1 August 1862	Wycombe Railway	High Wycombe-Thame	Broad
4 October 1864	Wycombe Railway	Thame-Kennington Junction	Broad
5 January 1873	East Gloucestershire Railway	Witney-Fairford	Standard
8 September 1873	Abingdon Railway/Great Western Railway	Abingdon Branch extended to new station at Radley	Standard
9 May 1890	Woodstock Railway	Woodstock Road (Kidlington)-Blenheim & Woodstock	Standard
3 August 1900	Great Central Railway	Culworth Junction-Banbury Junction (to goods and passengers	Standard

Removal of Broad Gauge

Date	Section
1 April 1869	Oxford mp64-Oxley, Wolverhampton
3 August-1 September 1870	Maidenhead-Thame-Kennington Junction
5-27 November 1872	Abingdon Junction-Abingdon
6 November 1872	Oxford mp64-Didcot

Closure Dates

Station or line	Service removed	Date
xford old station	Passenger	1 October 1852
	Goods	26 November 1872
xford Rewley Road station	Passenger	1 October 1951
ard	Goods	5 April 1984
idlington-Woodstock	Completely	1 March 1954
/itney-Fairford	Completely	10 August 1962
arnton-Witney	Passenger	10 August 1962
	Goods	11 November 1970
adley-Abingdon	Passenger	9 September 1963
	Goods	30 June 1984
ennington Junction- Princes Risborough	Passenger	7 January 1963
	Goods	1 May 1967

Railmotor Halts

	Opened	Closed
Great Western Railway		
Wolvercot platform	1 February 1908	1 January 1916
Hinksey halt	1 February 1908	22 March 1915
Abingdon Road halt	1 February 1908	22 March 1915
Iffley halt	1 February 1908	22 March 1915
Garsington Road Bridge halt	1 February 1908	22 March 1915
Horspath halt (1)	1 February 1908	22 March 1915
Horspath halt (2)*	5 June 1933	7 January 1963

* This new halt was built some two chains nearer Oxford.

	Opened	Closed
London & North Western Railway		
Port Meadow halt	20 August 1906	25 October 1926
Woolvercot halt	9 October 1906	25 October 1926
Oxford Road halt	9 October 1906	25 October 1926
Oddington halt	9 October 1906	25 October 1926
Charlton-on-Otmoor halt	9 October 1906	25 October 1926
Wendlebury halt	9 October 1906	25 October 1926

Bibliography

The Oxford Worcester & Wolverhampton
    Railway, S. Jenkins and H. Quayle.
The Witney & East Gloucestershire Railway,
    S. Jenkins.
History of the GWR Vol 1 and 2, E. McDermot.
Clinkers Register of GWR Halts and Platforms,
    C. Clinker.
The Woodstock Branch, R. Lingard.
The Oxford, Thame & Princes Risborough
    Branch, R. Lingard.
The Oxford to Cambridge Railway Vol 1,
    B. Simpson.

The Oxford Canal, H. Compton.
The Great 'Great Western', W. J. Scott.
The Railway Age, C. Andrews.
The Armstrongs of the Great Western,
    H. Holcroft.
Regional History of the Railways of Britain,
    Thames and Severn, R. Christianson.
Regional History of the Railways of Britain,
    Chilterns and Cotswolds, R. Davies.
Railways of the Cotswolds, C. Maggs.
Locomotives of the GWR Parts 1-13, RCTS.

A considerable amount of information has been obtained from the *County of Oxford* magazine. This journal was produced by the City of Oxford Locomotive Club which operated from 1953 until 1962. Regular meetings were held at a local college and trips were organised to most steam locomotive depots in the country. Swindon Works, for example, was visited approximately every seven weeks, and the author personally visited Swindon on over 30 occasions with the club. A regular membership of between 50 and 80 'lads' had many enjoyable visits to these steam depots throughout the years.

The *County of Oxford* magazine wa produced on a regular basis giving all of th local engine sitings at Oxford and in th surrounding area. What was once schoolboys' pastime in producing such magazine, has now proved to be an invaluabl record of locomotive workings in the Oxfor area between 1955 and 1962, the period ove which it was published. The author ha fortunately been able to obtain a copy o almost every issue produced.